FIFTY
NEW
DEVOTIONAL
PROGRAMS

FIFTY
NEW
DEVOTIONAL
PROGRAMS

Ernest C. Andrews

BAKER BOOK HOUSE
Grand Rapids, Michigan

PHOTOLITHOPRINTED BY CUSHING - MALLOY, INC.
ANN ARBOR, MICHIGAN, UNITED STATES OF AMERICA

PREFACE

All Scripture quotations are from the King James Version. All other quotations are given credit where the source is known. Other hymns may be substituted and programs rearranged to suit time and need. It is hoped that these brief meditations will be helpful for the many occasions where a devotional program is needed.

E. C. Andrews

CONTENTS

1 TURNING OVER A NEW LEAF

Central Aim: To consider the past year with a view to improving oneself in the new.

Prelude: "Ring out the Old, Ring in the New"

Call to Worship: "This month shall be unto you the beginning of months: it shall be the first month of the year to you."—Exod. 12:2

Hymn: "Another Year Is Dawning"

Scripture: II Timothy 1:12

Prayer: O God, may we begin this year with an abiding faith in Thee and receive grace to continue it in Thy favor with Thy guidance for all our doings.

MEDITATION

As the old year ends and a new one comes in, all of us are inclined to speak of this time as an opportunity for "turning over a new leaf." We long for the place called "The Land of Beginning Again."

> *I wish there were some wonderful place*
> *Called the Land of Beginning Again,*
> *Where all our mistakes and all our heartaches,*
> *And all of our selfish grief,*
> *Could be dropped like a shabby coat at the door,*
> *And never put on again.*
>
> Louisa Fletcher Tarkington

What we often fail to realize is that in God's grace and assurance we have such a place. "Behold, I set before you an open door" is the promise. We must make it our business to go through that door in this new year. No one has a good

1

garden who will not cultivate it and keep out the weeds. No one can have a finer self who is not willing to pay the price in daily action.

Yet as we stand before this open door of a new year with its unknown possibilities, sorrows, and successes we hesitate as did the one in "The Gate of the Year":

> *And I said to the man who stood at the gate of the*
> *   year;*
> *"Give me a light, that I may tread safely into the*
> *   unknown";*
> *And he replied:*
> *"Go out into the darkness and put thine hand into*
> *   the Hand of God.*
> *That shall be to thee better than light and safer*
> *   than a known way."*

Minnie Louise Haskins

The apostle Paul had no such hesitation because he had an assurance. "I know" . . . a person. Paul had reached out beyond himself to Christ, his Savior and Lord. Christ was the one in whom he had an all-absorbing attraction and joy. The focus of his life went past the soiled and treacherous things of earth to the One who he believed could transform not only himself but also a lost world. Jesus said, "For what is a man profited, if he shall gain the whole world, and lose his own soul?" (Matt. 16:26).

> *What is a man profited if he knows the age of rocks*
> *   but not the Rock of Ages?*
> *What is a man profited if he knows the way the*
> *   heavens go, but not the way to go to heaven?*
> *What is a man profited if he knows the price of*
> *   pearls but not the Pearl of Great Price?*
> *What is a man profited if he sees all other stars but*
> *   not the Bright and Morning Star?*

Paul had an assurance. "I know" . . . a persuasion. Immediately after his Damascus Road experience, Paul's enemies began to seek his life. Even the Christians found it difficult to accept him fully. Did that stop him? slow him down? cause him to hesitate? Not at all. *He was persuaded.* The Christ he had met was able to keep him and all that he had committed to Him. Paul wrote to the Romans, "And we know that all things work together for good to them that love God, to them who are the called according to his purpose" (8:28). He does not say that all things in this world are good, or that all things that happen to a person are good, but rather that they work together for good.

This new year may be one of the hardest years of your life, but it may also be one of the best. It can mark a period of Christian growth as you look back on the old year with its neglected kindnesses, unsettled grudges, unkind words, and unstraightened curves. Turn over the new leaf, begin the new year with a clean slate, put your hand in the hand of God and walk through the open door with assurance.

Hymn: "Father, Let Me Dedicate"

2 BLANK CHECK

Central Aim: To explore God's providential care for His children.

Prelude: "This Is My Father's World"

Call to Worship: "Every good gift and every perfect gift is from above, and cometh down from the Father of lights, with whom is no variableness, neither shadow of turning."—James 1:17

Hymn: "Showers of Blessings"

Scripture: Philippians 4:19

Prayer: Accept our praise, Holy Father, for all the provision of our needs that Thou hast made. Help us to cast our cares upon Thee with full knowledge that Thou dost care for us.

MEDITATION

What if someone should hand you a blank check with his name signed to it and say, "Fill it in for whatever you need"? If you know him and his financial standing, you might do so immediately. If he is unknown to you, you would probably check with the bank on which it was drawn to see how much it would be good for. In essence, this verse is just such a blank check handed to us.

Consider how personal Paul makes the source: "my God." Not just the God of Israel, or the God of the covenant, or the God of our fathers, but *my* God. He is a God of personal experience and intimate fellowship—a God who not only promises but who can deliver on His promises. Do you know this God?

Charles Steinmetz, the electrical genius, never received a fixed salary from his sponsors. They simply furnished him with a book of blank checks. Whatever his needs—great or small—he simply filled in the amount on a check drawn on General Electric and signed his name to it. It was always honored.

In the same manner we need only to fill in God's blank check to supply our needs. Notice how positive this promise is: "shall supply."

Is the need salvation? Then the check reads, "Look unto me, and be ye saved, all the ends of the earth."

Is the need comfort? Then the check reads, "Let not your heart be troubled, neither let it be afraid."

Is the need strength? Then the check reads, "He giveth power to the faint."

Is the need security? Then the check reads, "Underneath are the everlasting arms."

Paul points out the provident fulfillment found in God's blank check: "all your needs." Notice that he says "needs"— not "greeds." Maclaren says, "The axiom of Christian faith is that whatever we do not obtain we do not require." But each of us does have needs that must be met. How lovingly God wants to take us into partnership with Him and provide us a flat guarantee that we will never be insolvent again.

The psalmist knew this. He claimed God's blank check when he said, "I shall not want."

I shall not want for rest—for "he maketh me to lie down in green pastures."

I shall not want for refreshment—for "he leadeth me beside the still waters."

I shall not want for forgiveness—for "he restoreth my soul."

I shall not want for companionship—for "thou art with me."

I shall not want for comfort—for "thy rod and thy staff, they comfort me."

I shall not want for anything in this life—for "surely goodness and mercy shall follow me all the days of my life."

I shall not want for anything in the life to come—for "I will dwell in the house of the Lord forever."

God's blank check is drawn on a supply that can never be exhausted: "according to his riches in glory." Can the ocean be emptied with a thimble? Can a bird use up all the oxygen in the air? Can a mouse eat up all the wheat in the world? Neither can we exhaust God's boundless supply for our needs. His riches are as endless as the universe or the varied needs of humanity, and He supplies them "according to" and not "out of." The distinction is this: If a millionaire is approached for a contribution to a cause and he gives five dollars, he has given out of his riches but not according to his riches. When Paul says "in glory" he puts God's riches above our reach, but when he adds "in Christ" he brings them all down among us.

Hymn: "Jesus Is All the World to Me"

3 HE'S A BRICK

Central Aim: To foster the truth that we all have our place in God's kingdom.

Prelude: "Have Faith in God"

Call to Worship: "For other foundation can no man lay than that is laid, which is Jesus Christ."—I Cor. 3:11

Hymn: "Trust and Obey"

Scripture: I Peter 2:5-8

Prayer: Loving Father, we are so weak and restless. Make us to realize that in Thee and through Thee we all have our place in Thy Kingdom.

MEDITATION

Have you ever heard the expression "He's a brick"? It is one of the highest compliments that can be paid to a person. The word was first used about 800 B.C. by a Spartan lawgiver named Lycurgus. An ambassador from another state asked Lycurgus why there were no walls about his city. He replied, "Oh, but there are, and if you will come with me I will show them to you." He led the ambassador to the field where his army was marshaled in battle array. Pointing to the ranks of men, he said, "There are the walls of Sparta and every man a brick."

In the same manner the Christian is a living stone in the building of a spiritual house. Such stones are drawn out of nature's quarry, they are cut and polished by the Spirit of the living God, and prepared for the place they are to occupy in God's master plan.

Stones are a common building material in Palestine because they are so plentiful. Let us translate the stone into brick (a building material more familiar to us) and think of every Christian in terms of a brick.

A brick may be of any color and shape. I have seen red, yellow, black, and white bricks and every shade of variation in between. Bricks come long and thin, short and squat, average, and various degrees in between. Just so, the living building material of God's spiritual house on earth comes in all sizes, all colors, and all shapes. This has always been true. The ancestry of Jesus contains Rahab the harlot and Ruth the Moabitess as well as the most royal of Jewish blood. In this is foreshadowed the truth that in Christ is neither bond nor free, neither Jew nor Gentile, neither male nor female. Neither is there any respect of persons with God.

Another thing about a brick is that it must be fired to be useful. Once while driving along a highway near Santa Fe, New Mexico, I saw a sight so interesting that I stopped to watch. A man was walking up and down in a pit about six feet by four and possibly eighteen to twenty inches deep. He was puddling adobe. Over to one side were row after row of adobe bricks baking in the sun. A short distance away was a house to which a room was being added. This was where the bricks were to be used. That adobe had to be heated and baked before it could be useful.

In like manner, we must pass through the fire of the Holy Spirit before we can be useful in God's kingdom building enterprise. We must also be baked in the crucible of experience. It is from a combination of these two that we emerge as dependable, no matter what the occasion, and loyal, no matter what the temptation. No one wants to use brick that dissolves when the rain comes, nor can God use us to the praise of His glory if we become weak and dissolve away when the storms of doubt and fear assail. Tested, tried, and proved, we become fit to be a part of the wall which rises on the sure foundation of Christ.

Likewise, a brick in any wall must bear a sustaining relationship to the cornerstone. God, the Master Builder, has laid the Chief Cornerstone; and from there every brick in the house of God gets its straightness, trueness, and design.

Finally, a brick is most useful when it is a part of the whole. Let us think for a moment of a brick wall being built. Each brick in its turn is cemented into place. But suppose one brick says, "No, I had rather not be a part of that wall. I'll just stay here and be a brick on my own." So he refuses to be used, to be a part of the wall. And so what happens? Either he gets kicked around and broken up or he becomes grassed over and lost to sight. The moral is plain for us all. The individual Christian is in his true place only when he is a part of the wall which is the church.

Hymn: "Faith Is the Victory"

4 TONGUE-TIED

Central Aim: To discuss the problem of loose tongues and un-Christian speech.

Prelude: "Now to the Lord a Noble Song"

Call to Worship: "Let your speech be always with grace, seasoned with salt, that ye may know how ye ought to answer every man."—Col. 4:6

Hymn: "Praise Him, Praise Him"

Scripture: James 3:1-12

Prayer: Give unto us the speech that betrays with whom we have been, and may it always reveal Jesus.

MEDITATION

It is a most embarrassing situation to be in the place of needing to say something and finding that there are no words. One man on such an occasion said, "Words fail me. I can only be Biblical and say, 'He was speechless.'" But most of the time our tongues are not tied. We use them too freely. The Associated Press carried a story one day about a boy, who in running home one wintry day in subzero weather, slipped on some ice and fell against an iron pole. His tongue hit the pole and instantly froze to it, so tightly that he couldn't even free it with the loss of some skin. With the cold wind pouring into his mouth, he couldn't breathe warm air on the pole to thaw his tongue loose. He wasn't released until police, summoned by his sister, thawed apart his tongue and the pole by the use of warm water. Our tongues do get us into trouble.

For the most part our tongues are not tied. Just a breath of scandal makes a conversation breezy for many people. Every man sins, but the most common sin of all is that of the tongue. Oscar Wilde said, "Your tongue is like a scarlet snake that dances to fantastic tunes." A bit controls a horse, a rudder controls a ship, and the tongue controls us. All are small in proportion to the weight they manage, but then it has been observed that a tongue three inches long can cut down a man six feet tall.

9

Our tongues are not tied when it comes to boasting. There is a boasting which is false—about ourselves. There is a boasting which is impossible, as in the matters of faith. But there is a boasting which is both true and possible. It is boasting in what God is and what He has done. It was while he was meditating on this that the psalmist exclaimed, "My soul shall make her boast in the Lord" (34:2).

Someone has said that one minute of keeping your mouth shut is worth an hour of explanations. Unfortunately our tongues are seldom tied when they should be. In 1646 an author by the name of Theodore Reinking faced execution because of a book he had written that offended King Christian IV of Denmark. The king offered Reinking the alternative of literally eating his words or being executed. What would you have done? Reinking tore his book to shreds, soaked it in soup, and ate it. But we do not have the opportunity to eat our words, even if we should dearly wish that we could. That which is in the well of our hearts is sure to come up and be poured out in the bucket of our speech.

Sometimes our tongues are too loose in the form of slander which burns up the reputation of another. Gossip has been defined as the art of saying nothing in a way that leaves nothing unsaid. Benjamin Franklin said:

> *Man's tongue is soft, And bone doth lack;*
> *Yet a stroke therewith, may break a man's back.*

Sometimes our tongues are too loose in the form of words which burn up trustfulness in other people. We hear a lot about Miss America or Miss Universe, but there are five other misses that cause much trouble. Let me introduce them. They are mis-information, mis-quotation, mis-representation, mis-interpretation, and mis-construction. And sometimes our tongues are tied when they should be loose. Silence is not always golden; on some occasions it may be just plain yellow—as when we do not speak to defend or correct as we should.

Our tongues are not tied. Therefore, how will we use them? Will they be used to the praise of God or to the cursing of men? Let us guard against leakage and loss of power that comes through hasty words unfitly spoken.

Hymn: "The Fight Is On"

5 FALL IN

Central Aim: To encourage church attendance and relate its value to our lives.

Prelude: "I Love Thy Kingdom, Lord"

Call to Worship: "And he is the head of the body, the church: who is the beginning, the firstborn from the dead; that in all things he might have the pre-eminence."—Col 1:18

Hymn: "The Church's One Foundation"

Scripture: Isaiah 6:1-8

Prayer: Teach us to honor and love the church even as Thou hast loved it and given Thyself for it.

MEDITATION

What happens when you go to church? Anything? Nothing? How often people respond to an invitation to attend a church service with the glib reply, "Oh, if I went the roof might fall in." Isaiah went to church and it did seem as if the roof fell in and the whole building was set to reeling and rocking with the presence of God.

Yes, *the roof just might fall in* on some people's self-righteousness. Every day begun and lived without faith in God must end with the cry of Romans 7:24: "O wretched man that I am." But every day begun and lived in faith will end with the victorious cry of Romans 8:37: "We are more than conquerors through him that loved us." These two chapters show us the two ways of facing life. In Romans 7, the word *I* occurs thirty-two times and the Holy Spirit is not mentioned once. In Romans 8, the *I* occurs only twice and the Holy Spirit is mentioned sixteen times.

The roof just might fall in on some people's contempt for the church. Paul asked the question of the Corinthians, "Despise ye the church of God?" (I Cor. 11:22). Some feel contempt for the church because in their sight it is so hopelessly behind the times. Perhaps so, but it is also the gateway to the future. Some hold it in contempt because it is so often wracked and torn by controversy. That is only too true; yet the church holds the key to eternal harmony. Some despise the church because "it is always asking for money." Why shouldn't it? Every organization asks for money, but no other one can equally offer treasures in heaven. Some despise the church because it seems to have so little influence in the community. That is often true. The church is overlooked or ignored. However, few people want to live in a community where there is no church. Some despise the church because, they say, "It is full of people like me." Of course it is. The only difference is that they want to do better than they are doing now.

The roof just might fall in on some people's lack of interest. In Numbers 10:29-33 there is a remarkable little story of how Moses said to his brother-in-law, "Come, and go with us and we will do thee good." And Hobab said, "I will not go." There is in human nature an instinct which balks at anything when its only recommendation is that it is good for him. Many are even persuaded that what is good for them is bound to have a bad taste. But when Moses changed his tactics and challenged Hobab to be the eyes of the Israelites on their journey to the Promised Land, Hobab got together his gear and went with them. Many individuals who have shunned the promises and privileges of the church are set afire by the challenge of souls to be saved and sins to be conquered.

The roof just might fall in on some people's procrastination. Myriads of excuses are offered in self-defense by those who do not attend church. The flimsiest I ever heard was expressed by a couple who said that they lived too far from the church to walk but too close to get the car out and drive.

Many seem to feel that there is no hurry to seek forgiveness of sins, to respond to God's love and grace, or to become a part of His church both visible and invisible. They have decided to wait until near the end of life and then be like the dying thief. To them I pose this question, "Which thief?" Do you despise the church or declare yourself for it?

Hymn: "The Kingdom Is Coming"

6 CHECK IT OUT

Central Aim: To provide a warning and a guide for self-measurement.

Prelude: "Give Me a Heart Like Thine"

Call to Worship: "For we dare not make ourselves of the number, or compare ourselves with some that commend

13

themselves: but they measuring themselves by themselves, and comparing themselves among themselves, are not wise."—II Cor. 10:12

Hymn: "Nothing Between"

Scripture: Psalm 26:1-2

Prayer: Lord, make us mindful of our tendency to minimize our weakness while maximizing our strength and goodness.

MEDITATION

We all need salvation from self-commendation. A young girl in England was applying for a position as a housemaid. She showed her recommendations to her prospective employer. After reading them, the woman said to her, "You certainly have some fine recommendations here." The girl replied in a pleased voice, "I'm glad you like them. I wrote them myself." It is hard for us to see our own worth clearly and without illusions. But few of us dare to make the proposal set forth by the psalmist: "judge me . . . examine me . . . prove me."

Whenever there is a plane crash of undetermined origin, pieces of the metal are sent to a laboratory for examination. Tests are made to see if the metal has failed; and if so, why. Similarly, the psalmist is anxious that God should take his examination into His own hands, to conduct it in His own way, and to submit him to such tests as would find out all his weaknesses, all his errors, and all his sins.

Do we dare to examine our own secret life—let alone permit God to do it? When the light of God falls into these secret places of ours, no wonder we jump as if we were jabbed. What every life needs is a yardstick that is always thirty-six inches, not occasionally twenty-two or thirty-two inches. We all tend to ease the strain of moral and spiritual effort by measuring ourselves against an easy comparison. But here is the true standard: "Until we attain to the measure of the stature of the fulness of Christ." Let us measure our smallness against His greatness, our selfishness against His love, and our faithlessness against His performance of the Father's will.

Do we dare to examine our home life? Sins have been tolerated in the home which we would be ashamed for outsiders to know about. It was little foxes that ruined the grapes, and little sins can ruin the happiness and harmony of the home.

Do we dare to examine our social ways? How we have acted in the company of our friends may reveal the secret of our failure as Christians.

Do we dare to examine our pride? An actor confided to some friends, "I used to be quite conceited. But my analyst cured me of that, and now I am one of the nicest guys in town." Pride can be so subtle that we lose our trust in the Lord and in the power of His might. It is false to say that a man who lives a righteous life has nothing to say for himself. But it is equally false to say that because you don't do certain questionable things, you have an inner life in harmony with the divine. Our overt actions don't touch the matter of motives or hidden desires.

Do we dare to examine our motives? It is a human right to have individual significance and dignity, to be "somebody." But the very basic human desire to count for something is a very different thing from the desire for mere prominence or V.I.P. rating for its own sake. Mazzini, the Italian artist, showed the right spirit when he wrote to a friend, "Pray for me that, before I die, I may be good for something." The Bible says, "I show unto you a more excellent way" (I Cor. 12:31). There is a more excellent way to be "somebody" in

15

the highest sense, to be a member of the greatest nobility on earth. Through faith in Christ we become both sons of and servants to the Most High.

If we submit ourselves to God's scrutiny and seek His will through His Word, we will not be holding inverted values but measurements of true value.

Hymn: "I'll Live for Him"

7 TRIED AND TRUE

Central Aim: To focus attention on the trustworthiness of the Bible.

Prelude: "Holy Bible, Book Divine"

Call to Worship: "I will meditate in thy precepts, and have respect unto thy ways. I will delight myself in thy statutes; I will not forget thy word."—Ps. 119:15-16

Hymn: "How Firm a Foundation"

Scripture: Psalm 12:6-7

Prayer: Lead us to marvel anew at Thy Word and its power to fill the needs of our lives. Help us to learn more of its living truths.

MEDITATION

That time of national life we call "golden" may be called the darkest by heaven. That age recorded as great in history may be lamentable in the sight of God. Great buildings, wealth, power, marble, jewels are but dust and ashes if there is no morality or virtue. One factor and one only can keep things in balance, and that is adherence to the Word of God. The words of men are the smoky fires of earth, but the words of God are the starry lights of heaven which never lead astray.

The Word of God has been tested, tried, and found true. It has been tested and tried in its conflict with worldly values. The Bible is truth opposed to all error, holiness opposed to all sin, good opposed to all evil. It is united in its testimony, accurate in its prophecies, distinct in its claims, reliable in its promises. In every test it has encountered with the world, the Bible has proved its worth. It is searching in its discernment but assuring in its message.

As it was with the divine Son, so has it been with the divine Word. Concerning Christ, the record is that He "endured such contradiction of sinners against himself" (Heb. 12:3). So also has the Word of God been tried by the contradictions of unbelief. As it was said of those who sought the life of the Christ child, "they are dead which sought the young child's life" (Matt. 2:20), so it can be said of those who have sought the destruction of the Word of God in times past. They were great thinkers and writers—men like Payne, Mirabeau, Hume, Renan, Voltaire, Mill, Ingersoll, Russell— but they are all dead; whereas the Bible lives on undefeated. The Bible has—to some men's satisfaction—been refuted, exploded, overthrown, and demolished; but somehow it just goes on increasing in circulation, influence, and power. Truly did Isaiah speak when he said, "The word of our God shall stand forever" (40:8).

The Bible has been tried by personal experience and found to be true. Jesus said to the Jews, "If I do not the works of my Father, believe me not" (John 10:37). So also can we test the Bible. According to the skeptics, the Bible is false in fact and philosophy and ought to make society selfish and barbaric. But it doesn't. One notable example is Pitcairn Island,

17

famous as the home of the descendants of the *Bounty* mutineers. It was once the scene of shocking crime, but it has become world renowned for the integrity and cleanliness of its people. Today it has no crime, no jail, and no police. What brought about such a change? Nothing other than the Word of God, exemplified by Fletcher Christian's Bible, still to be seen today in a chapel on the island.

The Bible has been tried in relation to man's moral and religious necessities and found to be true. Multitudes have made it the foundation of their convictions, the fire of their warmest love, the law that undergirds the conscience, and the support for every duty and difficulty. Every manner of person has tested Scripture and found it to be just what he needed and all that he needed. Jesus said, "The works that I do, bear witness of me" (John 5:36). So also does the Bible make its claim that by its fruits do we know it.

All of us value those things that have been tried and found true and workable. In sickness we want a tried and proved medicine. In trouble we want a tried and true friend who will stand by. In bad weather we want a dependable place of safety. The Bible comes to us as a Word that has been tried, offering to us a sure and happy guidance, a restraint from the temptation of evil, an aid in the pursuit of good, consolation in the hour of sorrow, peace in the midst of tumult, and victory in the hour of death. The Bible has never failed anyone in generations past who put his confidence in its truth, and it will never fail us.

Hymn: "Break Thou the Bread of Life"

8 JUST BETWEEN US

Central Aim: To show our need for a mediator and to magnify Jesus as that mediator.

Prelude: "Jesus Saves"

Call to Worship: "Wherefore he is able also to save them to the uttermost that come unto God by him seeing he ever liveth to make intercession for them."—Heb. 7:25

Hymn: "He Is Able to Deliver Thee"

Scripture: Job 9:25-35

Prayer: We thank Thee that Thou hast remembered man in his weakness and provided him with a mediator.

MEDITATION

Job admits the dimensions of God's power, saying that the world is His from tip to toe. He can make it or break it, adorn it or ravish it, and who will say no to Him? And what standing could Job have in a trial? If a summons could be served on the Almighty, it would be to no purpose. If God was to answer, He would still turn a deaf ear to every complaint. Job saw himself as alone and sick of life but still tormented by God. For what possible good? For what profit, or pleasure, or reason?

Then a thought of stupendous dimension invades Job's mind. God was so transcendent and infinite and he himself was so earthbound and finite; but what if there was a third party, a mediator who would stand between him and God, putting his hand on both? What if an arbitrator or umpire would come forward to terminate their estrangement, make them intelligible to one another, and reconcile their differences into the bond and unity of peace? Job never knew how close he was; but his instinctive cry for a God in human form, for a mediator between God and man, is an unconscious prophecy of Christ who stands between us and God to effect our reconciliation.

This craving for someone to stand between us and God is awakened by an awareness of sins. No man can be his own pope. Ceremonies do not satisfy. The ritual of all religions and the moralism of all mortals are in vain. Against the absolute will of God every human attempt at clearance miscarries.

This craving for someone to stand between is also awakened by our suffering. Job cried out, "O earth, cover not my blood, and let my cry find no resting place. Even now, behold, my witness is in heaven, and he that vouches for me is on high. . . . And he will maintain the right of man with God like that of a man with his neighbor" (16:18-19, 21). Poor Job! There is no hint of divine sympathy, no hint of loving purpose in affliction. There is no knowledge, no dream of Christ. Yet beyond the miseries of the present pain and weeping eyes, he discerns the face of a heavenly witness. His blood will be shed in death, but his last breath will not mean the closing of his case. A mediator does wait to affirm his righteousness.

In Job's day and ours, the heart of man seeks someone who will maintain his right and speak up for him in his hour of need. In a latter day, Paul affirmed this when he declared, "For there is one God, and one mediator between God and man, the man Jesus Christ" (I Tim. 2:5).

This craving for a mediator is awakened by the resurrection hope. Job said, "For I know that my redeemer liveth, and that he shall stand at the latter day upon the earth: and though after my skin worms destroy this body, yet in my flesh shall I see God" (19:25-26). Job has already posed the question, "If a man die, shall he live again?" He now takes a brave leap of faith past the dark of a thousand contradictions to answer yes. Man may have to wait until eternity for the explanation of some things, but he can die knowing he has a living redeemer in heaven. God is God and man is man; so there needed to be one between—a God-man. There is such a man—the man Jesus Christ who came from glory and returned to glory.

There is a man in glory who stands as our mediator, pleading the royal law of redemption—the death of the just for the unjust.

There is a man in glory who walked alone that we should never be forced to walk alone.

There is a man in glory who is the center of Scripture. Everything in the Old Testament points to Him; everything in the New Testament proceeds from Him.

There is a man in glory whose name stands as the guarantee of our needs, whose promise is, "Ask, and ye shall receive, that your joy may be full" (John 16:24). Hallelujah!

Hymn: "I Will Arise and Go to Jesus"

9 DON'T BLAME ME

Central Aim: To pinpoint the responsibility of sin.

Prelude: "O Happy Day"

Call to Worship: "For there is not a just man upon earth, that doeth good, and sinneth not."—Eccles. 7:20

Hymn: "There Is Power in the Blood"

Scripture: James 1:13-16

Prayer: Remind us again, O God, that we cannot shift the responsibility of our sin to anyone else. Lead our heart to its confession for the good of our soul.

MEDITATION

The mother was understandably upset. The lamp lay in shattered fragments on the floor. As she opened her mouth to speak, one little boy forestalled her with the words, "Don't blame me." And the other boy quickly added, "Nor me either." Isn't it marvelous at what tender ages we learn to offer an excuse for ourselves?

Sin and temptation come with many faces and bearing many names. Is it not true that every one of us experiences such assaults upon our soul? Sometimes the temptation is like a barrage of artillery fire and we seem likely to succumb from the sheer overwhelming fury of it. At other times it comes like a sniper in some secret hiding place trying to pick us off. Again, it may be like an anesthetic, silently lulling us into sleep and oblivion of all that is about us. So we are tempted and so we sin. But when we sin can we say, "Don't blame me?" If we are not to blame, then whom shall we blame?

Shall we blame our fellowman? Husbands and wives frequently blame each other for their marital failure. Church workers blame others for failures which they themselves have helped to cause. Businessmen excuse bad practices because the competition is doing it. Adam accused Eve of leading him astray in the garden. "The woman thou gavest me, she. . . ." Aaron blamed the people for the sin of the golden calf, and Pilate put the blame on the multitude when he gave up Christ to be crucified.

If we are not to blame, should we blame our passions? We come into this world the product of our ancestors. But the past does not determine our fate, it only determines our trial. Pope wrote:

> *On life's vast ocean diversely we sail,*
> *Reason the card, but passion is the gale.*

What about Adam? He had a perfect environment. There was no alcohol to make him drunk, no drugs to destroy his will, no cursing to degrade his character, no adultery possible—and yet he sinned. Joseph was in a place so adverse to goodness that nine out of ten persons would have succumbed; but he withstood his environment by asking, "How then can I do this great wickedness, and sin against God?" (Gen. 39:9). Paul looked at the circumstances and wrote, "There hath no temptation taken you but such as is common to man: but God is faithful, who will not suffer you to be tempted above that ye are able; but will with the temptation also make a way to escape, that ye may be able to bear it" (I Cor. 10:13).

If we are not to blame, should we blame God? Adam did. When he said, "The woman thou gavest me...," he was indirectly including God as the cause of his sin. He seems to say, "If you had not given me this woman...." Robert Burns said it:

> *Thou know'st that Thou formed me*
> *With passions wild and strong;*
> *And list'ning to their witching voice*
> *Has often led me wrong.*

In essence he blames God for his conduct because God made him. But this will not hold true. God is holy; therefore evil has no charm for Him. God loves man and seeks only his good. Therefore if God were to tempt us with evil, He would cease to be good, cease to be holy, and cease to be God.

If we were perfectly honest, shouldn't we blame ourselves for our sin? James thinks that we should and puts the responsibility for sin squarely on us. "Stop deceiving your-

23

selves" is his command. Man is tempted by his own evil desires.

Almost every public building has signs that say "Exit." And the way out of sin and temptation has been clearly marked for our guidance. It is to be so mastered by Christ that we become the master of our temptations.

Hymn: "Yield Not to Temptation"

10 PROOF OF THE PUDDING

Central Aim: To lead into a deeper understanding of the work and assurance of the Holy Spirit.

Prelude: "Spirit Divine, Attend Our Prayer"

Call to Worship: "And I will pray the Father, and he shall give you another Comforter, that he may abide with you forever."—John 14:16

Hymn: "Holy Spirit, Faithful Guide"

Scripture: Galatians 3:1-5

Prayer: Thanks be unto Thee, O God, for the Holy Spirit who convicts and converts and convinces us ever anew.

MEDITATION

"The proof of the pudding is in the eating," said Cervantes. And to that Paul would agree. He is surprised that the Galatians have not thought through the implications of their manner of salvation. He does not really charge them with having no intelligence, but rather with a failure to use what they have. To put it into modern terminology, Paul is saying,

"You are not even using your heads. Examine your experience for the proof of how you were converted."

The proof of the pudding was in seeing Christ as crucified for sin. The words "evidently set forth" are a translation of a Greek word meaning "placard" or "poster." Paul is not talking about any art poster that has been nailed up, but to his public preaching of Christ crucified. In the power of the Spirit, his preaching is so vivid, so graphic, that his audience feels as if they could see and almost touch the Christ.

In the comic strip "Li'l Abner" there is a man with an evil eye who can throw a half, whole, or double whammy. That is amusing to us, but the evil eye was a fearful superstition to the Greeks. It may be partly serious and partly humorous when Paul asserts that someone throwing an evil-eyed whammy on them must be the cause of their thinking about leaving the gospel.

The proof of the pudding was in how the Spirit and His gifts were received. The most unmistakable evidence of God's favor and plainest guarantee of redemption is the gift of the Spirit, for the spirit is the essence of all God's good gifts to men. As a man gives good gifts to his children, so does the heavenly Father give the best of gifts to His children. The Spirit is the Christian's ally in the time of need, the source of comfort in the time of sorrow, and the guardian of the righteous way. No one can ever say that the Spirit comes as a reward for works. He comes only as the gift of grace to the response of faith.

When Paul says that God "ministereth to you the Spirit," he is using a word that means to supply abundantly. Without the Holy Spirit all we can say is "I think" or "I hope," but with the Spirit we can say "I know." I once saw a poster in a stock room at a department store which showed a man stooping over a large package. On the poster were the words, "If it's heavy, get help." Just so, when our problems are heavy and our burdens are great, we can call on the Spirit.

If we begin our Christian careers by the work of the Spirit, we can be sure that they will be completed by the work of the Spirit. We can never begin in the Spirit and end in works, for it is the Spirit all the way. John the Baptist said we would be baptized with or in the Spirit. Baptized means to dip or immerse. Have you, by chance, ever dyed anything? I once dyed a shirt another color. I immersed it in that dye, and when it came out the dye had penetrated all through the fabric. Even so, a Christian is a person who is dyed through and through with the Spirit. The whole color of his life is changed by the Spirit, and he is penetrated with the Spirit. Our salvation is no halfway house—part Spirit and part works. As it is begun by the Spirit, so it will be completed by the Spirit.

Hymn: "The Holy Ghost Is Here"

11 PEACE CORPS

Central Aim: To show how God has called all Christians into the ministry of making peace.

Prelude: "Ye Must Be Born Again"

Call to Worship: "How beautiful upon the mountains are the feet of him that bringeth good tidings, that publisheth peace; that bringeth good tidings of good, that publisheth salvation; that saith unto Zion, Thy God reigneth!" —Isa. 52:7

Hymn: "There Is Power in the Blood"

Scripture: II Corinthians 5:17-21

Prayer: Lord, make us to be publishers of Thy peace even as we ourselves have been partakers of it.

MEDITATION

Her eyes sparkling with enthusiasm, the new graduate from college confided that she had joined the Peace Corps. "Just think, " she bubbled, "I am going to Africa for two years." That was hard for me to envision of a girl who had never been away from home, except during college semesters. But the vision of the Peace Corps had caught her, and so to Africa she went to a very happy and profitable two years.

The Peace Corps was suggested by President Kennedy as a means of carrying the message and meaning of America to underdeveloped countries by a person-to-person contact of a self-help nature. The idea has vision, imagination, challenge, and appeal. But it is not a new idea. The first Peace Corps came over nineteen hundred years ago when Jesus said to His disciples after His resurrection, "Peace be unto you: as my Father hath sent me, even so send I you" (John 20:21).

When Paul addressed the church at Corinth, he pointed out to them that they were a Peace Corps. God's Peace Corps was founded on the common denominator of salvation through Jesus. Unless a person became a transformed person, where old things had passed away and all things had become new, he could not be a member of the Peace Corps. For if one has no peace, how can he speak peace with persuasion?

Every person in God's Peace Corps has the same work and the same motivation. The motivation is that we have been reconciled to God; the old barrier of enmity has been broken down and peace is reigning in its place. The work is that we have been made the hands, heart, feet, and mouth of Jesus to carry that message of reconciliation to others.

That message of peace is that God was in Christ, reconciling the world to Himself, forgiving our sins and trespasses, no longer holding us accountable for them because of Christ's completed work. Like the old-time Western Union delivery boy, our job is to deliver the message. We are not to argue with it, or change it, or debate it, but deliver it.

According to various polls, upward of 90 percent of the people in America believe in God. But not nearly so many believe in a Biblical concept of sin. Before any person can be saved, he must be conscious of sin. A pig is a pig but he doesn't know he is a pig. A man is a man and he knows he is a man. This is the vital difference, and this is why the word to man is "Repent."

Our work in God's Peace Corps confers on us a new title: ambassadors for Christ. Notice Paul's stress. Christ is not present with us in the flesh today. But we are available, we know Him, and we pray you ourselves—in His absence and on His behalf—be reconciled to God. An ambassador is one who represents his country in a foreign land. He is not a native of that land, but his allegiance belongs back home in the land he represents. He serves to transmit the messages of his government to the government of the country to which he is assigned.

The Peace Corps was to be a person-to-person ambassadorship. God's Peace Corps also has that relationship. His message is: "Neither is there salvation in any other: for there is none other name under heaven given among men, whereby we must be saved." (Acts 4:12). And all those who hear and believe gain a new standing—righteousness with God.

Hymn: "Are You Washed in the Blood?"

12 HARD AS A NAIL

Central Aim: To expose the dangers of becoming hard-hearted.

Prelude: "Must Jesus Bear the Cross Alone?"

Call to Worship: "Verily I have cleansed my heart in vain, and washed my hands in innocency."—Ps. 73:13

Hymn: "My Soul, Be on Thy Guard"

Scripture: Hebrews 3:7-8

Prayer: Remind us anew that our hearts are deceitful and that we must ever be on guard lest they lead us astray. May they be always tender to Thy call.

MEDITATION

How do you describe something as being hard? When I was just a boy phrases like "hard as nails," "hard as a brick," and "hard as a pine knot" all entered into my vocabulary. The French author Guy de Maupassant described a character in one of his novels as having fingers as hard as lobster claws. Helen Green described someone as being as "hard as a 1907 prune." The New Testament uses two Greek words to describe the hardening of the heart. Follow these words and a perfect picture of a heart in the process of becoming as hard as nails emerges.

Paul wrote to the Ephesians about the Gentiles "having the understanding darkened, being alienated from the life of God through the ignorance that is in them, because of the blindness of their heart" (Eph. 4:18). The word for "blindness" is the same word in the Greek as "hardened." It is the word used to describe the mending of a broken bone. The calcium deposit that repairs the break of a bone is harder than the bone itself. This is the example of a conscience that has become as hard as nails. It has ceased to perform its functions because it is so calloused that no sensitivity remains. Immorality does not disturb because the conscience has petrified. This is why Dillinger was able to make the astounding remark, "I never did a wrong thing in my life."

Paul wrote to the Romans, "Or despisest thou the riches of

29

his goodness and forbearance and longsuffering; not knowing that the goodness of God leadeth thee to repentance? But after thy hardness and impenitent heart treasurest up unto thyself wrath. . . " (Rom. 2:4-5). When a man's heart is tender toward God, he sings, "Bless the Lord, O my soul, and forget not all his benefits." When it is not tender, he takes everything from and gives nothing to God—not even the time of day. There are multitudes with hearts as hard as nails who cry, "God be merciful" but who never say, "God be praised." There is no music on earth so pleasing to God as the thankful songs of His saints.

Jesus took His disciples to task when they misunderstood His warning about the scribes and Pharisees. He said, "Perceive ye not yet, neither understand? have ye your heart yet hardened?" (Mark 8:17). Have you ever watched the area where sidewalks are being poured? The contractors are usually hard put to keep children from leaving the imprint of their hands or feet in the soft cement. But after awhile, it doesn't matter. The cement has set and the walks are hard. No impression can be made in them. Jesus was trying to teach His disciples a lesson but they did not understand; their minds refused to receive the impression. Isaiah was told that he was to go and tell the people, "Hear ye indeed, but understand not; and see ye indeed, but perceive not" (Isa. 6:9). It was because they had so hardened their hearts that no impression could be made on them.

When Paul preached in Ephesus there were some converts, but there were also many who became hard as nails and would not believe. They even spoke evil of the Christian life before the multitudes. As in every age, there is so much that is wrong with the church today that it is easy to forget what is right about it. Before anyone begins to downgrade the church and the Christian fellowship of community that is expressed through it, he had better reconsider.

To have a heart that is becoming as hard as nails can only be accomplished by resistance to the Holy Spirit. That tugging at our hearts is the Holy Spirit seeking to lead us out of our stubbornness, hardening hearts, and sin.

Hymn: "Who Is on the Lord's Side?"

13 DOES IT PAY?

Central Aim: To explore the basis of our worship of God, that it may be made pure.

Prelude: "All Hail the Power"

Call to Worship: "God is a Spirit: and they that worship him must worship him in spirit and in truth."—John 4:24

Hymn: "Crown Him with Many Crowns"

Scripture: Job 1:9-11

Prayer: Purify us, O God, that our worship of Thee may be in an acceptable spirit. Purge us of all unworthy motives and beliefs, that we may serve Thee for Thyself alone.

MEDITATION

"Does it pay to do that?" or "What's in it for me?" has been a question long asked. Because it is so rooted in human nature, it spills over into our religious thinking. Why do we worship God? from habit? from social pressures? as a matter of insurance both for the here and the hereafter? because we love Him? or because there is the prospect of worship being a good investment that pays off?

Satan believed that Job's motive in worshiping God was just that—it pays to serve God. In one sense of the word that is true. There is a blessedness in doing right. But to believe that doing right guarantees blessedness is a far different thing and only one step removed from trying to put God in one's debt because of right doing. Remove Job's motive, Satan challenged, and he will be no more pious than the next man.

There is a time honored proverb that says, "Honesty is the best policy." In that proverb is expressed the verdict of mankind down through generations of personal experience. But are you an honest man if you are honest only as a matter of expediency? Is honesty right? If it is, then we are being honest only when we are honest whether it pays or not, simply because honesty is right.

In the same manner, godliness is profitable; but we are not to be godly for the sake of profit. We are not true Christians as long as we follow Christ only for what we can get, anymore than were those Galilean crowds who followed Him for a time because they ate of the loaves and were filled. When we truly worship God we follow Him for Himself and would rather go with Him to prison and death than to live in a world without Him. Love cannot be love it if stops to ask, "What's in it for me?" Besides, what would God's grace be worth if it could be had for a price? How secure could any relationship be where this world's goods were bartered for loyalty? Purchased devotion is too weak to survive.

In the Old Testament, tremendous stress is laid on the rewards of religion. While the Jews interpreted it in far too narrow a manner, there is a connection between what we do and the results of what we do. "Oh, it doesn't matter" is easily said, but it's not the whole truth. There is also both a consequence and a bonus built into life. Sometimes we receive something we think we do not deserve, and it may be a help or a hurt because it touches our lives from events in which we had no part.

In the Old Testament, temporal disaster is threatened as the punishment for sin; and worldly prosperity is promised as the reward of goodness. Job was being led to see that worship and goodness must be served for their own sake. Elihu quotes Job as saying, "It profiteth a man nothing that he should delight himself with God" (34:9). In a way, that complaint is true. Serving God may not pay off any better than not serving Him. God is impartial and does not play favorites.

Does it pay to serve God? Yes, because of the alternative. Jesus said, "For what is a man profited, if he shall gain the whole world, and lose his own soul? or what shall a man give in exchange for his soul?" (Matt. 16:26). We may look at someone who is cheerfully unconcerned, uncommitted, uninhibited, and feel twinges of envy. But what is there to envy? Would you exchange a heart at peace and a life rich in love for a heart raging with anger and lust and a life of pride and greed? Would you exchange the hope of glory for the allurements of time?

Does it pay to serve God? Yes, because of who He is and what we are. The psalmist said, "O come, let us worship and bow down; let us kneel before the Lord our maker. For he is our God; and we are the people of his pasture and the sheep of his hand" (95:6). There is a joy in doing right and loving God freely for Himself.

Does it pay to serve God? Yes, it has always paid. Not in the coin of the realm, but in the fruits of the Spirit.

Hymn: "Holy, Holy, Holy"

14 TRUE FACTS

Central Aim: To explore the promise and meaning of eternal life.

Prelude: "Where We'll Never Grow Old"

Call to Worship: My sheep hear my voice, and I know them, and they follow me: And I give unto them eternal life; and they shall never perish, neither shall any man pluck them out of my hand.—John 10:27-28

Hymn: "I Know That My Redeemer Liveth"

Scripture: John 3:36

Prayer: Our Father, we thank Thee for the assurance of our continuing life and its joys forever. Help us to live now as never dying.

MEDITATION

When I was in college, I had a professor who always caught us up short if we used the phrase "true facts." He would always say, "If it is a fact, it is true. If it is true, it is a fact. Let the word *fact* stand alone." But when two words are put together like this, it does add an emphasis, and in other languages is a device often used. When we come to think about the everlasting or eternal life found in Christ, nothing less than such emphasis seems adequate, for it is a life of duration as well as quality. It is life that has begun in God, and not even what we call death can hinder or harm it. It is life that begins the moment we trust Christ, it is a life that has no end.

It is a true fact that eternal life is the promise of God. "And this is the promise that he hath promised us, even eternal life" (I John 2:25). "But you promised me," is the cry that often follows a broken promise. And we poor

34

mortals do break our promises, either because we have promised what we do not have the power to deliver, or because we just don't want to keep them. But this is never true of God. He has both the power to keep His promises and the will to do so. God promised Noah safety—and He delivered on that promise. He promised Abraham a son—and He delivered. He promised Israel a land of their own—and He delivered. He promised us eternal life—and if we will take it, He will deliver.

It is a true fact that eternal life is the gift of God. "And this is the record, that God hath given to us eternal life, and this life is in his Son" (I John 5:11). He has given us life in Christ forever and He does not take away what has been claimed.

It is a true fact that eternal life demands a knowledge of God. "And this is life eternal, that they might know thee the only true God, and Jesus Christ, whom thou hast sent" (John 17:3). If we wish to enter into life eternal we must never be too busy with the things of time to think about eternal things.

Two little girls were discussing their families. One asked the other, "Why does your grandmother read the Bible so much?" The other replied, "I think she's cramming for her finals." If we do not know Jesus as Savior, our finals will be a time of rude awakening as we discover that our grades are not good enough for us to be promoted by the greatest Teacher of them all.

It is a true fact that eternal life demands obedience to God. "And being made perfect, he became the author of eternal salvation unto all them that obey him" (Heb. 5:9). We can never enter into complete intimacy and unity with someone with whom we continually differ.

It is a true fact that eternal life demands loyalty. "My sheep hear my voice, and I know them, and they follow me" (John 10:27). No man who goes his own way can enter into eternal life. Eternal life is for the man who in complete loyalty takes the way of Jesus Christ. When Cardinal Wolsey was being led away to the Tower, he remarked, "If I had served my God as faithfully as I served my king, He would not have deserted me."

The French author Guy de Maupassant has a story titled "The Necklace." It is a story about a necklace—assumed to be made of diamonds—that was borrowed, lost, and replaced by many years of hard work, when in reality the original was only paste. Whatever we may be working for, whatever our goal in life may be, if in the end we do not have eternal life, then our lives will have been spent for paste—an imitation of the real thing.

Hymn: "When the Roll Is Called up Yonder"

15 MAN ALIVE

Central Aim: To point up the usefulness to God of a man who is spiritually and physically alert.

Prelude: "Onward, Christian Soldiers"

Call to Worship: "Run ye to and fro through the streets of Jerusalem, and see now and know and seek in the broad places thereof, if ye can find a man, if there be any that executeth judgment, that seeketh the truth; and I will pardon it."—Jer. 5:1

Hymn: "Faith of Our Fathers"

Scripture: Job 22:2

Prayer: O God of ages, lead us to be the kind of person with the quality of spirit that will make us useful to Thee.

36

MEDITATION

"Man alive," we say when our spirits are stirred by some thrilling tale of adventure. "Man alive, I wish I could have been there." Eliphaz was thinking in terms of the adventurous man, the mighty man, the valiant man, the powerful man, the hero, the man who is a leader, the man who is the best and most vigorous specimen of manhood when he asked the question: Can such a man be useful to God? And to Eliphaz the answer is a resounding no. He brushes aside even the thought of such a thing. But the work of Christ is the adequate answer to Eliphaz. What was the sense of the shedding of that precious blood if man is of no consequence to God? There is no basis or justification for redemption except on the premise that man is so precious to God that the death of Christ was judged not too high a price to pay for his redemption. We are redeemed for God's glory—redeemed to be men alive unto the soul-stirring adventure of following Jesus across the earth and through the years.

Man alive, we can be profitable to God when we have conviction. What kind of conviction? A conviction of sin that says, "I know that in me, (that is, in my flesh) dwelleth no good thing" (Rom. 7:18). When a man is ready to uncover his sins, God is always ready to cover them with forgiveness. All that a man says of grace, of the power of the gospel, of the utter necessity of Christ rests on his own admission of personal bankruptcy. And he knows that no lawsuit is ever necessary to collect the wages of sin. The man who is alive to God knows that it is far better to say, "This one thing I do," than to say, "These forty things I dabble in." No man's religion has ever drawn interest by laying it away in cold storage.

Are you a doctor?—then live Christ as the Great Physician.

Are you an electrician?—then live Christ as the Light of the world.

Are you a carpenter?—then live Christ as the Chief Cornerstone and Sure Foundation.

Are you a student?—then live Christ as the Incarnate Truth.

Are you a teacher?—then live Christ as the One having the answers of life.

Are you a laborer?—then live Christ as the Master Craftsman.

The saving experience of Jesus is far too rich and many-sided to explore in isolation. We hear a lot said today about "togetherness." Paul was a leading exponent of togetherness in its best meaning. He refers to his companion Christians as fellow athletes, fellow heirs, fellow partakers, fellow servants, fellow soldiers, fellow workers, fellow citizens, fellow helpers, fellow prisoners, fellow sufferers, fellow sharers, fellow yokebearers, and fellow imitators of Christ. Men are most alive and most profitable to God when they are laborers together. The only time Paul went anywhere alone, he could hardly wait until the rest of his party arrived.

Let none ever consider himself as having made any recompense to God for His grace. "When ye shall have done all those things which are commanded you, say, We are unprofitable servants: we have done that which was our duty to do" (Luke 17:10). Man alive, have we even risen to that adventure?

Hymn: "Rise Up, O Men of God"

16 PRESCRIPTION NEEDED

Central Aim: To prepare Christians for revival by presenting God's requirements.

Prelude: "Jesus, I Come"

Call to Worship: "Wilt thou not revive us again: that thy people may rejoice in thee?"—Ps. 85:6

Hymn: "Lord, Send a Revival"

Scripture: II Chronicles 7:14

Prayer: Lord, help us to follow Thy Word and its wisdom, that we may be revived in the church and in all of life's activities.

MEDITATION

The greatest need of our day is revival. I do not speak of a week of preaching morning and night. I do not speak of a simultaneous crusade, by whatever name, or of a central meeting. I speak of that great revival of the Spirit where the Word of God means something; where lost souls become precious to those who know God; where Christians recover their first love; where the church becomes precious and elect; where we forget who we are and what we are with all the sin that goes with it and remember that we are only sinners saved by grace. Revival will never take place as long as we trust publicity more than the power of the Holy Spirit, or promotion more than prayer. Publicity and promotion have a place, but the Spirit and prayer must have preeminence. Revival can come—God says so.

Take a look at the people of revival: "my people." Revival always begins with Christians; others have nothing to revive. Christians are called believers because they believe in Jesus sufficiently to give Him power of attorney over their lives. They are called disciples because they are willing to be taught and trained by Jesus. They are called followers because they forsake other things for the companionship of Jesus. They are called brothers because they are members of the family of God, and no member of the family wishes to be happy at the expense of the misery of any other member.

Take a look at the price of revival. God sets before us four requirements which must be met before revival comes.

1. "Humble themselves." Pride has always been listed as one of the deadliest of sins. We are as proud as Paul in his persecution or Peter in his pledge of faithfulness. Proud are we—too proud to admit sin, too proud to show emotion, too proud to take a lower seat, too proud to fill the needs of the church.

2. "And pray." For prayer to be more than prattle, it must come from a heart broken for sin and from sin; from a heart concerned about the will and majesty and dominion of God. It must come from a heart of compassion over the lost and straying, from a heart that cares less for self and more for others.

3. "And seek my face." This means, "Be as I am." We do that by being holy, separated to the Lord. It means to turn away from the unfruitful works of darkness and to work the works of God while it is yet day. It means to clean off your mud spattered light that it may shine in a world of darkness.

4. "And turn from their wicked ways." God knows all there is to know about us for He looks on the heart. He knows the lust, hatred, deceit, jealousy, blasphemy, pride, and evil thoughts that tear our heart out, corrode our service to Him, dryrot our testimony, ruin our effectiveness, and rob our soul of its fresh, glowing love for Jesus.

Has God set too high a price for us to pay? Is His prescription too bitter for us to swallow? Had we rather die than to follow the doctor's orders?

Take a look at the promise of revival. God knows the sickness of sin and how to make us well when we follow His prescription.

"Then will I hear"—mark you—"then": not until we have followed the course laid out. This is a principle that has never been altered. "Let the wicked forsake his way, and the unrighteous man his thoughts: and let him return unto the Lord, and he will have mercy upon him; and to our God, for he will abundantly pardon" (Isa. 55:7).

"Will forgive their sin"—no one but God can; but, strangely, He is the last one we want to come to. Just as many people defer an operation, preferring to live a dragging existence, so there are many who will not come to the great Physician for the sickness of their soul.

"Will heal their land"—and whose land ever needed healing more than ours?

"If," God says. I wish that "if" were not there, but it is. It implies that a decision must be made and it can go either way. The prescription is given. Will we take it and fill it?

Hymn: "I Must Tell Jesus"

17 SERVICE CALL

Central Aim: To explore the ways and means by which God calls us to commitment.

Prelude: "Ready"

Call to Worship: "If any man serve me, let him follow me; and where I am, there shall also my servant be: if any man serve me, him will my Father honour."—John 12:26

Hymn: "Follow On"

Scripture: Isaiah 6:1-8

Prayer: Help us to hear Thy calls, O Lord, and give us the grace and wisdom to follow Thee.

MEDITATION

There is a Negro spiritual that states a vital necessity:

I know the Lord, I know the Lord,
I know the Lord has laid His hand on me

If one is to be used of the Lord, then he must know the Lord; and he will rightly know the Lord only when the Lord has laid a hand on him in a personal encounter, in an individual experience. Jesus said, "Ye have not chosen me, but I have chosen you, and ordained you, that ye should go and bring forth fruit, and that your fruit should remain" (John 15:16). Yet on man's side there is always the matter of obedience, and this obedience is what makes him an effective servant of the Lord.

God's call to Isaiah was very clear, practical, and definite. It is the fashion of the world to think of prophets and dedicated religious workers as being impractical, dreamers of dreams, or visionaries out of touch with the realities of life. This is as wrong as the world usually is.

Isaiah could point to the map of life and say, "It was there that I saw God. It was in the year Uzziah died."

Jeremiah could say, "It was in the thirteenth year of the reign of Josiah that I heard the word of God."

Ezekiel could say, "It was in the thirtieth year, in the fourth month, in the fifth day of the month, that I saw the heavens open while by the river Chebar."

Paul could say, "It was on the road to Damascus, close to the city and about midday that I saw the light."

God's call is never standardized. Paul, Isaiah, Ezekiel had visions, Jeremiah did not. Some can point you to the time or take you to the place, others cannot. But the voice of God is no less real if it comes through a friend, a song, or a church.

An artist was painting a picture of a woman out in the night, thinly clad, tossed by a tempest and hard driven, with a baby hugged to her breast. As he painted, he suddenly threw down his brush and said, "God help me; why don't I, instead of painting pictures of lost people, go and help them myself!" He did go and help them. The last twenty-five years of Alfred Tucker's life were spent as a missionary to Uganda.

Just as no man can tell God in what manner his call must be, neither can he tell God where or for what purpose he is to be called. Only one attitude of the soul is permissible and that is, "Here am I, send me." With that frame of attitude, regardless of what comes or goes, the soul will still sing, "Hallelujah, the Lord God omnipotent reigneth."

Ruskin said, "The more I think of it, I find this conclusion more impressed upon me, that the greatest thing a human soul ever does in this world is to see something and tell what it saw in a plain way."

And what are purified lips for, if not to speak the unsearchable riches of Christ?

And what are opened eyes for, if not to tell the glory of God beheld through them?

"Send me"—this is the mark of every committed servant of the Lord. Every vision must pass into vocation or it will be lost.

There must be human response to divine appeal. A man must perform the essential act of submission before he receives a commission. What a joy for a cadet when he receives his commission and insignia. What a joy for a Christian when he receives his call and commission:

> *Salvation! Oh, Salvation!*
> *The joyful sound proclaim,*
> *Till earth's remotest nation*
> *Has learned Messiah's name.*

Hymn: "Where He Leads Me"

18 GOOD MORNING

Central Aim: To reaffirm the joy and triumph of the resurrection.

Prelude: "Christ the Lord Is Risen Today"

Call to Worship: "Blessed be the God and Father of our Lord Jesus Christ, which according to his abundant mercy hath begotten us again unto a lively hope by the resurrection of Jesus Christ from the dead."—I Peter 1:3

Hymn: "He Lives on High"

Scripture: Matthew 28:1-10

Prayer: We thank Thee, our Father, for the joy and assurance that is ours through the resurrection of Jesus from the dead.

MEDITATION

Some mornings are late in getting started. We oversleep for one reason or another. Some mornings are slow in getting started. One thing after another interrupts and it seems that the day's schedule will never get under way. Yet when we meet one another, the greeting and response is still routinely "Good morning." Is it courtesy, or good manners, or habit? Or is there something deeper—far deeper?

Matthew records that the women came to the tomb as it was beginning to dawn. Mark says of this event that it was "very early in the morning." It was the morning of the resurrection. The hope that died on the cross and was laid to rest with Jesus in His grave sprang to a new life on this morning.

At least three times the Lord had told His disciples in what manner He would die, assuring them that on the third day He would rise again. He said it coming down from the Mount of Transfiguration, "Tell the vision to no man, until the Son of man be risen again from the dead." (Matt. 17:9). He said it in the upper room, "Yet a little while, and the world seeth me no more; but ye see me: because I live, ye shall live also" (John 14:19). He said it on the way to the garden, "But after I as risen again, I will go before you into Galilee" (Matt. 26:32). But His disciples had forgotten this until Jesus met them on the day of the resurrection. There were no dramatics, no fanfare—just a natural, common greeting: "All hail." What had begun as a sorrowful day had turned into a bright, beautiful, good morning.

It is a good morning because we have the assurance of peace. Saved by the Lord, we can forget our sinful past, we can forgive ourselves, and we can face today and tomorrow with peace of mind. This is what the hymn sings about:

> *Peace, perfect peace, in this dark world of sin.*
> *The blood of Jesus whispers peace within.*

Pity those who never have a good morning because they do not know Jesus and the power of His resurrection. Be glad that you have heard the Savior say, "It is all forgiven—every fall and every fault, every omission and every commission.

There is nothing now between me and thee."

It is a good morning because we have the assurance of a radiant spirit. Jesus came from eternity to tell you and me that all power and authority is given to Him in heaven and earth. He came to tell us we were not left as orphans in this world, for the Holy Spirit is our Comforter. His power is available for our needs and for victorious living. Who has any excuse for a defeated spirit?

It is a good morning because now we have no confidence in the abilities of the flesh.

It is a good morning because sin's barriers and burdens are lifted.

It is a good morning because we have access to all power, to all wisdom, and to all glory.

It is a good morning because we have an assurance of the future. Without the resurrection of Jesus, "they also which are fallen asleep in Christ are perished (I Cor. 15-18). Michael Faraday, the scientist, was asked just before his death, "What are your speculations about the future?" He replied, "Speculations? I have none. I am resting on certainties!"

The resurrected Christ is the "first fruits of them that slept," and all who now believe will follow in His train. Because Christ is risen, we know that even on the blackest of days, the God who raised Jesus from the dead is also able to see us through. One of Luther's enemies said to him, "Tell me: when the whole world turns against you—church, state, princes, people—where will you be then?" Luther replied, "Why, then as now, in the hands of Almighty God." Good morning! A word of greeting with a world of meaning.

Hymn: "Christ Arose"

19 HEARTTHROB

Central Aim: To relate our life's attitudes and work to our worship experience of God.

Prelude: "Crown Him with Many Crowns"

Call to Worship: "O come, let us worship and bow down: let us kneel before the Lord our maker."—Ps. 95:6

Hymn: "O Worship the King"

Scripture: Psalm 16

Prayer: Lord, make us realize that our worship of Thee is molded by our attitudes and work and the experiences we have with Thee through life.

MEDITATION

However much or little the psalmist had, it was, he believed, to be from the Lord. He pondered, "The Lord is the portion of mine inheritance . . . thou maintainest my lot" (16:5). Paul said it to the Romans like this, "And we know that all things work together for good to them that love God" (8:28).

Not all things are "good," by any means. But the belief in a personal providence does make all things work together for good. With such faith, although our little world may shake and turn dark, there is enough security to make us stable and enough light to read the signs of God's guidance. This man became sure of God—not because of a miracle or supernatural sign, but by God's common providence in his life. Such an experience with God in the common ventures of life—birth, education, marriage, work, death—left him with a heart throbbing full of love and devotion toward God.

He knew the Lord in a personal way, "Thou art *my* Lord."

47

God has no grandchildren, for every generation must make its individual choice of becoming a son or not. It is not enough that God is the God of my father, He must be *my* God if I am to have a glad heart. The psalmist repudiated all other gods, saying, "In thee do I trust." He had no expectations from any other source and trusted God for all. What can a person possibly lack if he possesses the Possessor of all?

Interestingly enough, it did not take signs or dreams, visions of angels or voices from heaven, for him to know the leadership of God in his life. His communion with God in day or night season made it a certainty in his heart. Is it possible that our faith is weak or our communication faulty when we ask God for a sign concerning His will?

It is small wonder that this man's heart throbbed with joy and gladness over the Lord for we read, "I have set the Lord always before me." The surest way to know ourselves is to set the Lord before us. We do not like to pick flaws in the self whom we love. We are us—and we stand by us. But when we measure ourselves by Jesus, we can see ourselves for what we really are. Constant contact with true greatness and goodness lifts even a small man, and for this reason we are admonished to "grow in grace." God is always going before us and beckoning for us to follow. The more we learn of Him, the more we discover there is to learn.

With the Lord before us, we also have a basis for hope. There are sufferings of this present time, but God is also in this present time as well as in the future. In this world we are often troubled about the future. Sometimes the shadows are deep and the pathway to the goal seems deep; but remember: if the Lord is before us, we are following after Him and going forward toward Him. Therefore, whatever the future may hold for us, it holds God—and that is enough.

With his knowledge of spiritual safety, it is to be expected that the psalmist's heart was throbbing with joy. "Thou wilt

show me the path of life; in thy presence is fulness of joy."
The path of life consists of doing the will of God. Eternal life
is not just future, it is also present and is bound up with
living in communion with God, doing His will, and growing
daily more and more into the image of His son. The path of
life will lead us through sorrow as well as joy. It will involve
the difficult and painful as well as the joyous and consoling,
but we need never doubt that its end will be the presence of
God and the eternal pleasures which are at His right hand for
evermore.

To talk as a friend with God, to question Him freely, to
frequent His house of worship, to be safe in the shadow of
His power, to be sure of His love and mercy, to be convinced
of His righteousness, to be certain of His providential care—
why shouldn't we have a heart throbbing with joy?

Hymn: "Come, Thou Almighty King"

20 FILL IT UP

Central Aim: To point out the need of the Spirit and how to
be filled with the Spirit.

Prelude: "Holy Spirit, Faithful Guide"

Call to Worship: "Create in me a clean heart, O God; and
renew a right spirit within me. Cast me not away from
thy presence; and take not thy holy spirit from me."—Ps.
51:10-11

Hymn: "Have I Grieved Thy Holy Spirit?"

Scripture: Ephesians 5:18

Prayer: Lead us, O God, into a deeper understanding of the purpose and power of the Holy Spirit for our lives.

MEDITATION

How often it is that we pull into a service station and say, "Fill it up." Containers exist to be filled. Nature abhors a vacuum and rushes to fill it with air. The spirit of man is no exception. As Adam Welch said, "You've got to fill a man with something." But with what will we be filled and how?

To be filled with the Spirit we must covet the best. Jesus said, "Blessed are they which do hunger and thirst after righteousness: for they shall be filled" (Matt. 5:6). If there is no desire, no sense of spiritual need, then there will be no concern and no effort to be filled by the Spirit. What keeps us from yielding to the Holy Spirit and seeking after His fullness?

Could it be some trivial issue? It is so much easier to give up what is respectable and considered completely right in our society than it is to give up what we know to be morally wrong.

Could it be that the price is not right? Thousands would rather get along on the drive and energy of natural ability and hard work than to surrender all to the Spirit.

Could it be that we have settled for a life of compromise—a life in which we have some of God and God has some of us?

Could it be that we cherish self too well? I read a striking statement about a person. It said, "He was too expensive for most of us." Self sniffs out slights and offenses. Self must be bowed to, honored, and spoken to. Self is hurt when someone else is chosen to sing or speak or pray or hold office. Such an ingrown spirit can never be Holy Spirit filled.

To be filled with the Spirit we must recognize our carnal

inclination. A Christian must always struggle against sin, and without Holy Spirit power he becomes a carnal Christian.

A carnal Christian lives a life of perpetual conflict and repeated defeat. He can't win for losing.

A carnal Christian lives a life of retarded growth. He is dependent on human friends and human help to see him through.

A carnal Christian lives a life of fruitlessness. He is more interested in television than evangelism, more interested in ball games than the Bible.

When we admit our failures and dependency on the flesh, the Spirit is prepared to fill us with His power.

To be filled with the Spirit, we must be cleansed. We cannot be filled with the Spirit if we are already filled with something else. I John 1:9 tells us: "If we confess our sins, he is faithful and just to forgive us our sins, and to cleanse us from all unrighteousness." Here forgiveness and cleansing are spoken of as two different acts. Forgiveness is God's attitude toward us, and cleansing is what He does for the condition of the soul. As a Christian we should not be so much interested in being abreast with the spirit of this age as in having the Holy Spirit of this age in our breast. When we are cleansed, then we can be filled.

To be filled with the Spirit, we must be committed or consecrated to God. What does it mean to be consecrated? It means that I lay my possessions, my potentialities, my personal friends on the altar. It does not mean I am made perfect according to the flesh, but it does mean that everything has been turned over to the Spirit and that His will becomes mine. It means for us to say along with the psalmist, "I delight to do thy will, O my God: yea, thy law is within my heart" (40:8).

If God has put a hunger and a longing in your life for spiritual betterment, then He intends to satisfy it.

If you are determined to have more in life than a feeble faith and a defeated practice, then to be filled with the Spirit is for you.

Hymn: "Have Thine Own Way"

21 MAKE A DATE

Central Aim: To make us more conscious of God's initiative in our lives.

Prelude: "Guide Me, O Thou Great Jehovah"

Call to Worship: "For this God is our God for ever and ever; he will be our guide even unto death."—Ps. 48:14

Hymn: "Lead, Kindly Light"

Scripture: Amos 3:3

Prayer: Create fresh within us, O Lord, a sense of wonder at Thy concern for us and its many manifestations of loving interest.

MEDITATION

"Can two walk together, except they be agreed?" (Amos 3:3). This passage has tremendous implications which are somewhat obscured by the translation of the King James Version. The Hebrew reads, "Can two walk together unless they have made an appointment?" This is also the translation given by a recent version. An appointment is an agreement to meet at a certain time and place. We make such dates all the time in business, in courtship, in recreation, and in sickness. By the same token, God has made some dates with us, which—if we are wise—we will keep.

God has made a date to meet us at the church. Matthew writes that Jesus said, "For where two or three are gathered together in my name, there am I in the midst of them (Matt. 18:20). It is important that we keep this date. The church is God's institution given to us for help in our weakness. Here we are bound together by the common denominator of Jesus Christ. He is the cause and purpose of our being in church. God meets us here in our worship and submission to His will.

God has made a date to meet us in prayer. "When thou prayest, enter into thy closet, and when thou hast shut thy door, pray to thy Father who is in secret; and thy Father who seeth in secret shall reward thee openly" (Matt. 6:6). Spontaneous prayer is good, but so are regular times set aside for prayer. It is true that God has given us freedom and spiritual manhood, but we never get entirely beyond the necessity of some rules. And there is no temptation so powerful or subtle as the one to neglect prayer. We often ask others to pray for us, and that is right and good. But no one can be deputy for us before the throne of grace. Hannah prayed and Samuel was born. Mordecai prayed and Haman hung on his own gallows. Elijah prayed and the Jordan parted. Paul and Silas prayed and the doors of time and eternity opened.

> *Come, let us rise at morning light*
> *And seek our God in prayer;*
> *Praise Him who kept us through the night*
> *And cast on Him our care.*

God has made a date to meet us at death, for "it is appointed unto man once to die" (Heb. 9:27a). Death is imposed that man might not be immortal in his sinful condition. Romans 5:12 says, "Death passed upon all men, for that all have sinned." An unsought bond on our part, death is one of the common ventures of our existence that no one evades. Every day we read of deaths in the obituary columns of daily newspapers. Every day the cemeteries are opening graves to receive bodies. It is a part of our human experience to know that death comes alike to rich and poor, powerful and weak, strong and sickly. Nor has God failed to remind us through His Word of this date we must all keep. The Bible says, "For dust thou art, and unto dust shalt thou return" (Gen. 3:19). It says, "There is . . . a time to be born, and a time to die." (Eccles. 3:2). It says, "Set thine house in order; for thou shalt die" (II Kings 20:1). It uses metaphors like wind, grass, flowers, a setting sail, to remind man of the brevity of time.

But supremely God has made a date to meet us at Calvary's cross. Paul wrote, "For God was in Christ reconciling the world unto himself" (II Cor. 5:19). We may see many beautiful cities; but we will never see the City of God, the new Jerusalem, unless we keep this date. We may see many of the varieties of trees on earth, but we will never see the Tree of Life unless we keep this date. We may view many of the celebrated rivers of earth, but we will never see the River of God flowing from the throne unless we keep this date. We may come in contact with and know personally many of the great people of earth, but we will never see the Lamb of God unless we keep this date.

There is only one of these dates that God will ever break. He will someday break the date of death, for Jesus is coming again and then death will be no more. Let us be watching for His glorious appearing.

Hymn: "He Leadeth Me"

22 HOT LINE

Central Aim: To lead toward a better prayer life by pointing out the value and need of prayer.

Prelude: "Did You Think to Pray?"

Call to Worship: "They that wait upon the Lord shall renew their strength; they shall mount up with wings as eagles; they shall run, and not be weary; and they shall walk, and not faint."—Isa. 40:31

Hymn: "I Must Tell Jesus"

Scripture: Hebrews 4:16

Prayer: Teach us not only how to pray but how to persevere in prayer that we may stay close to Thee.

MEDITATION

When Jess Gorkin, editor of *Parade* magazine, first proposed a "hot line" between Washington and Moscow, many people were skeptical. But in time it became a reality and it has proved its worth on many occasions. After all, there is nothing like being able to go directly to the top and having direct communication between the principals involved.

God has done just that for us. He has so arranged the universe and our place in it that we always have direct contact with Him. God is always at the other end of our "hot line" and always "answers the phone." John said, "And this is the confidence that we have in him, that, if we ask any thing according to his will, he heareth us" (I John 5:14).

The Bible breathes a spirit of prayer, and in it the prayer life of godly men and women is set before us. The value and need of prayer are pointed out on many pages of the Word. Many tributes have since been offered to its power:

Prayer moves the hand which moves the world.—J. A. Wallace.

Trouble and perplexity drive me to prayer, and prayer drives away perplexity and trouble.—Melanchthon

Embark on no enterprise which you cannot submit to the test of prayer.—Hosea Ballou

How can He grant you what you do not desire to receive?—Augustine

Religion is no more possible without prayer than poetry without language, or music without atmosphere.—James Martineau

Prayer will make a man cease from sin, or sin will entice a man to cease from prayer.—Bunyan

We all pray at some time or other. But most praying is done with superficial haste. Our minds are allowed to wander away from the subject, even while our mouths are uttering the words. Such praying is without thought or self-examination and open to question as to whether it is effective at all. Since our prayer is coming directly to the throne of God, it should be with the deepest sincerity.

How often have you been guilty of playing at praying? Do you think that the King of the universe is delighted to hear words pronounced with a flippant tongue and a thoughtless mind? Paul said we should continue "instant in prayer," meaning that we should be steadfast and regular in prayer. He also gave the exhortation to "pray without ceasing." Such exhortations are necessary because of our inclination to be spasmodic and uncertain in our prayer life. Almost anything can break the "hot line" between God and us. Such breaks of communication with God are harmful to our souls and a hindrance to obtaining power through prayer. How can we prevail with God when we lack the perseverance to maintain a dialogue with Him? John Newton said:

Then let us earnest be,
And never faint in prayer;
He loves our importunity,
And makes our cause His care.

Look on prayer as it really is—an art. I slipped into a prayer meeting one morning at one-thirty. Down toward the front of the chapel a man began to pray. Fifteen minutes later he closed his prayer. Not once in that time had he hesitated, faltered, or repeated himself. That man had mastered the art of praying. Had he not disciplined himself, had he not devoted much time with a degree of dedication, he could never have approached the throne of grace with such boldness, such grace, or such joy.

Yes, we have a "hot line" to God. But its use is left up to us.

Hymns: "Teach Me to Pray"

23 NO PARKING

Central Aim: To point out the danger inherent in our failure to grow in grace."

Prelude: "O for a Closer Walk"

Call to Worship: "Thou art worthy, O Lord, to receive glory and honour and power: for thou hast created all things, and for thy pleasure they are and were created."—Rev. 4:11

Hymn: "Give of Your Best"

Scripture: Genesis 19:17-21

Prayer: Father, forgive us where we have failed in faith to follow Thy leadership to a higher ground of grace and knowledge.

MEDITATION

"No parking." You do not have to travel far on a city street or a highway to see that sign. If a motorist ignores a "No Parking" sign and parks anyway, he may receive a ticket with its penalty. Neither can anyone park by the side of the road of life without paying a price. There is a moral demand to move on that is written into the world in which we live. When we become static we also become stagnant.

The story of Lot is the story of a man parking with his lowest ambitions. Because of Abraham, God sent a message to Lot to get out of the city of Sodom, not to stop on the plain, but to go to the mountains and live. In plain language God was saying, "Don't make the mistake of parking on or near your past. Make a clean break and move out toward your potentiality." But Lot began to plead in prayer with God for a lesser place, and so the curtain of holy history goes down with Lot parked in a dirt cave near the little town of Zoar in the foothills between the plain and the mountains. God answered his prayer, but Lot lost.

Lot lost his possessions. This was in reality the least of his losses, but it was for these that he gave up so much else. Lot was like many men today who, if they admire anything outside of themselves, it is success. They admire the smart operator, the man who gets by, the man who "beats the game."

Lot lost his home, family life, and part of his family. Today every home is teaching and distributing some brand of religion. Parents who say, "I'll let him choose later" are sowing the seeds of irreparable loss. They are doing what amounts to granting "kitchen privileges" to a toddler. Your children soon master the family's key words and parrot the family party line. What they hear offhand around the house is gospel to them.

Lot lost his wife. Surely he disliked losing his wife, but assuredly she was no help to him morally or spiritually.

Lot lost his separation. Worldly companionship can cor to live a life separated from the world.

Lot lost his sense of moral values. If a spark falls on ice—nothing happens; if it it falls on marble—nothing happens; but if it falls on gasoline—there is explosion, disaster, and death. In the same manner is the careless heart hit by the spark of temptation. Some people live in a dirty world and like it because they are dirty inside. If the heart is impure, everything that comes to or from it will be tainted. Lot became drunk and committed incest. Cancer will not cause a man to murder his wife, but liquor will. Heart disease will not place a man behind prison bars, but liquor does.

Learn the lesson of Lot that his dangers and his needs are ours also. Of course it is much easier to stay where we are and be comfortable with our position as it is. But there is not and never has been a divine provision for a parking place on the highway of life.

Hymn: "Higher Ground"

24 OLD GLORY

Central Aim: To rethink the positive values of patriotism and its symbols.

Prelude: "O Beautiful, My Country!"

Call to Worship: "Therefore thus saith the Lord; Ye have not hearkened unto me, in proclaiming liberty, every one to . . . his neighbor: behold, I proclaim a liberty for you, saith the Lord, to the sword, to the pestilence, and to the famine; and I will make you to be removed into all the kingdoms of the earth."—Jer. 34:17

Hymn: "America the Beautiful"

Scripture: Psalm 119:45

Prayer: Lord, make our hearts to rejoice in our country and its liberties and guide us that we may be diligent to preserve our freedoms for ourselves, our fellow countrymen, and our posterity.

MEDITATION

What is your flag? Is it just a piece of cloth dyed red, white, and blue and artfully arranged into a beautiful array of stars and stripes? Is it just a symbol that all good citizens display in front of their homes on days like Independence Day, Memorial Day, Washington's birthday, or Lincoln's birthday?

It is a symbol. But we must never forget the real things for which it stands. It represents a free people—with freedom from oppressive fear, with freedom to worship according to the dictates of one's own conscience, and with the freedom to think for oneself. It represents a republic "of the people, by the people, and for the people" that has given us a place of honor among the nations of the world.

The colors of our flag were chosen with purpose—red, white, and blue. Red—the color of blood—stands for life, vitality, action, and courage. White—the color of purity—symbolizes honor, grace, and cleanliness. Blue—the color of peace—stands for justice, fidelity, and peaceful ideals. These colors should be more to us than mere chemical tints on a

60

piece of cloth. They should represent to us all that is the best of our country. Charles Sumner said, "The very colors of our flag have a language. Red for valor; white for purity; blue for justice. And all together, bunting, stripes, stars and colors, blazing in the sky, make the flag of our country, to be cherished by all our hearts, to be upheld by all our hands."

It is disturbing, therefore, when some American people burn the flag, or dishonorably use it, or refuse to salute it. It is not a piece of cloth that is being despitefully used, it is the whole idea and purpose of America which has given them a home. Certainly we all have rights. But every right, or privilege, also has a corresponding responsibility or obligation. When we maturely meet our obligations, the matter of our rights usually is resolved also.

Old Glory was first flown on August 3, 1777. Made by Betsy Ross from some drawings given to her by General George Washington, the flag was made of strange components. A soldier's shirt produced the white, a woman's petticoat contributed the red, and a captain's coat the blue. In the intervening years changes have been made only to the field of stars, with one being added for each new state.

Founded on the fierce desire for freedom, nurtured by the ardent glow of patriotism, blessed of God with abundance, America has prospered and given generously of herself. She is my country and my home. If I cannot honor her and her flag, then I should seek another home. Is there any better flag than the red, white, and blue?

Hymn: "My Country, 'Tis of Thee"

25 HE'S A SQUARE

Central Aim: To secure a decision to live for Christ right now.

Prelude: "Jesus Calls Us"

Call to Worship: "I will cry unto God most high; unto God that performeth all things for me."—Ps. 57:2

Hymn: "I Am Thine, O Lord"

Scripture: Psalm 15:1-5

Prayer: Lord, in the midst of all that is changing, remind us anew that Thine eternal principles will never change.

MEDITATION

The group of boys stood looking at the retreating back of one of their number who had left. Then said one in disgust, "He's a square. Come on, let's go." "Square"—a good, wholesome word that has been twisted and distorted out of all resemblance to what it once meant. "Square" used to mean trying to be fair, honest, straight. It meant that you didn't cheat, or shave the corners, or goof off, or live beyond your means. It meant that you respected the law—both moral and civil. It meant that you did not sacrifice principles on the altar of expediency, that you could be trusted to do the decent thing.

Today "square" is a word that is applied in derision to those who refuse to be conformed to cult standards, who cling to the ideals of the Christian religion, who insist on the elementary dignity and self-respect of a human being. Is it possible that you are a square? If so, you are in good company, for the Bible is full of notable squares.

The man in this Psalm would be called a square. How much squarer can you get than speaking "the truth in his heart," doing no "evil to his neighbor," honoring "them that fear the Lord" and shunning those who do not, and swearing "to his own hurt, and changeth not." Probably no higher ethical concept of conduct is put forth in the Bible than this picture of a man who is walking uprightly.

Joseph would be called a square by this sex crazed age. A more perfect situation for the inevitable to be inevitable could not be devised. Consider the elements: a young man of passionate age, in a strange land, far from the restraints of home and family; an older infatuated woman, experienced in worldly ways; a husband away on business; the privacy of a home. But Joseph preferred to take his stand with the squares than to become an adulterer.

Moses would be called a square by this luxury-loving age. He had a name that would open the doors of the highest Egyptian society as the son of Pharaoh's daughter. He was trained in all the wisdom of that day, he had a position of power and authority, and he had all the comforts and luxuries that wealth could buy. Yet he turned away from it all to become the God-chosen leader of a mob of slaves. How square can you get? We are constantly confronted with a choice of values. Moses, square that he was, made the choice that has given him the position of lawgiver for all mankind.

Jonathan would be called a square by this expediency-at-any-price age. The son of the king, he knew that David would take his place on the throne. But instead of being bitter about the chances of fate, or being consumed with jealousy of David, he took the opposite course. He loved David, shielded him from his father, spied for David in the household of his father, counseled David as to the best course of action, fed him in exile, and tried to protect both his father and David from anything rash. How square can you get? But he did it because he was a friend to David.

Daniel would be called a square by this liquor-loving, self-indulgent age. Daniel refused the king's diet of rich food and wine. He was so square that he wouldn't even take a cocktail to relax. He was required to attend the state banquets where the liquor flowed freely, but he couldn't be made to drink. When the time came that the king needed a new prime minister, it wasn't a good-time Charlie, or a social drinker, or a yes-man that he selected. It was Daniel, the square.

God is still looking for squares who know the score and follow it. Satan is still singing his siren song of selfish indulgence. And man is forever at the fork in the road.

Hymn: "Living for Jesus"

26 WHAT A DAY!

Central Aim: To encourage the hope that is in the second coming of Christ.

Prelude: "There's a Great Day Coming"

Call to Worship: "For the Lord himself shall descend from heaven with a shout, with the voice of the archangel, and with the trump of God: and the dead in Christ shall rise first."—I Thess. 4:16

Hymn: "One Day"

Scripture: Philippians 3:20-21

Prayer: O Lord, glorious is Thy promise of returning. Strengthen our hands and hearts by that blessed hope.

MEDITATION

"What a day," we say as we come in at evening, sink into a chair, and kick off our shoes. We say it because it has been a day that has filled us with weariness by its demands and trials. But there is a day coming when all weariness will flee and joy eternal will reign. The Christian is not a settler here on earth. He is a pilgrim, but not a tramp; for a tramp is aimless while a pilgrim has an altar in his heart and a destination in his head. Just as Philippi was a colony of Rome, so are the Christians a colony of heaven. As such, we belong to a far-off homeland and wait with expectant longing for the day when King Jesus will come and fetch us home.

What a day it will be when He comes and this lowly body is changed. Truly it is a body bearing the marks of its limitations and weaknesses. It is the seat of human failure—the unwilling flesh which betrays the ambitions of the willing spirit. Just as automobiles have built-in obsolescence, so this body has locked-in limitations that doom it to death. But that is not the end. For in the day of His coming our deathless spirits will be clothed in a body fashioned in power and beauty like the resurrection body of the Lord. It will then reflect the new nature which we now have by faith and we will be brought to completion as a Christian.

What a day it will be when Jesus defeats the forces of nature that take this body of ours back to the dust from where it came. No man has ever defeated these forces, but Jesus will be able to do so. The obedience of nature has already been manifested when the winds and waves obeyed His words, "Peace, be still."

What a day it will be when Jesus brings the unbelieving hearts of men to subjection. Love has already proved to be the key that unlocks the restraints of men and sets them free. Love so amazing, so divine, demands and gets man's best and man's all.

What a day it will be when Jesus conquers spiritual wickedness in high places, prompted by the prince of the power of the air. Can Jesus truly conquer this fierce foe? Indeed— He already has. When the disciples of Jesus returned from their tour of Galilee with their reports, Jesus said, "I beheld Satan falling." Where is the sting of sin, the law, and death when Jesus is the victor over all?

> *Jesus shall reign where'er the sun*
> *Doth his successive journeys run;*
> *His kingdom spread from shore to shore,*
> *Till moons shall wax and wane no more.*

What a day it will be when He comes. To deny that He is coming again is to fail to understand the cross of Jesus. The ultimate outcome can never be in doubt. Sin will be uprooted. Suffering will cease. Disease will be banished. Rebellion will be put down. We have an immense curiosity as to what will happen next and when. The Bible tells us only that the day is coming. It is given without date so that we may live now as if He was coming today.

Hymn: "What If It Were Today?"

27 LISTEN TO ME

Central Aim: To point out our need of salvation.

Prelude: "Blessed Redeemer"

Call to Worship: "Look unto me, and be ye saved, all the ends of the earth: for I am God, and there is none else."—Isa. 45:22

Hymn: "Glory to His Name"

Scripture: Isaiah 49:1

Prayer: Heavenly Father, lead us to understand our nature and our need of forgiveness. Give us wisdom and faith to trust in Jesus as the sinner's only Savior.

MEDITATION

Have you ever heard a mother say to her child, "Listen to me"? Or heard someone in the midst of a heated discussion claim attention by saying, "Now you listen to me"? It is apparent that we must often use this expression, for I have heard children use it with the emphasis on the personal pronoun, "Listen to *me*." Isaiah seeks the attention of those to whom he speaks and calls for them to listen to his words. Have you ever stopped to consider how God has His means of saying, "Listen to me"?

When God drove man out of Eden, He was saying, "Listen to me. Sin is serious." Joseph knew that sinning was serious business and refrained from it, saying "How then can I do this great wickedness, and sin against God?" (Gen. 39:9). David knew that sin was serious and almost despaired, crying "Take not thy holy spirit from me" (Ps. 51:11). Peter knew that sin was serious and wept bitterly because of his betrayal of his master. God knew the seriousness of sin and knew that

67

man must be made conscious of it. Sin is the seed of all subsequent fruits of grief and pain. Sin stuns our sensibilities and leads us into rebellion against our sovereign God. It is serious indeed.

When God opened the Red Sea, He was saying, "Listen to me. I am sufficient for all your needs." We never walk alone; for His promise is, "I will not fail thee, nor forsake thee" (Josh. 1:5). We are never without comfort for "The Lord is my shepherd; I shall not want" (Ps. 23:11). We are never without adequate resources; for the promise is, "My grace is sufficient for thee" (II Cor. 12:9). We shall never be utterly cast down, for "underneath are the everlasting arms." (Deut. 33:27). We are never without protection; for we are "as the apple of his eye" (Deut. 32:10), and who hurts us, hurts God. If we grow weak it is He who "giveth power to the faint" (Isa. 40:29). Is it relief from tensions we need? His answer is, "My peace I give unto you: not as the world giveth, give I unto you" (John 14:27).

Why do we limp when we should be leaping? Why do we cower when we should be courageous? Why are we puny when we should be powerful? Is it because we do not take God at His promise to supply our needs? For us, God would cause the skies to give up their stars and the earth to give up her treasures. Paul, quoting Isaiah, expressed what he knew and felt God would do: "Eye hath not seen, nor ear heard, neither have entered into the heart of man, the things which God hath prepared for them that love him" (I Cor. 2:9). Sometimes God's supply comes through the fire, sometimes through the flood, but always through the blood.

When God sent the cloven tongues of fire flashing on the day of Pentecost, He was saying, "Listen to me. You are now ready to go." Go where, Lord?

Go—into the highways and hedges surrounding the freeways of life and death.

Go—into the fields that are white and ready for the harvest.

Go—after the least one of these my brethren, after the lost, after the last one.

Go—with the greatest of all great news—"Christ died for our sins."

God calls us to listen because Sinai and Calvary are tuned to the realities of life where we live. God calls us to listen, for faith and salvation come by hearing. "Listen to me" has ever been His call, and for the good of our souls we must do so.

Hymn: "At Calvary"

28 THAT REMINDS ME

Central Aim: To show that God is still the source of comfort for our souls.

Prelude: "Blessed Assurance"

Call to Worship: "I, even I, am he that comforteth you: who art thou, that thou shouldest be afraid of a man that shall die, and of the son of man which shall be made as grass?"—Isa. 51:12

Hymn: "All the Way My Saviour Leads Me"

Scripture: John 14:26

Prayer: Thou art our rock and our refuge, O Lord; and we beseech Thee for Thy comfort for our hearts.

MEDITATION

Shortly after World War I a man bought a number of surplus gas masks. They were delivered to his place of business by a red-headed soldier. Due to a lack of demand, over the years these gas masks were gradually pushed farther and farther back into the storeroom. Indeed, the man quite forgot that he ever had them in his store. After the outbreak of World War II a group of school girls came into his store one afternoon and asked for gas masks. At first he told them that he had none. Then he hesitated, glanced again at one of the girls, went to the back of his storeroom, rummaged around, and brought forth the gas masks. What had made him remember those masks? Why, that girl with the red hair, of course. "That reminds me," we say; and we do need to be reminded.

In a time of so much frustration, fear, and pessimism *we need to be reminded* that God is still on His throne. That is the rallying cry which John wrote from the isle of Patmos to the persecuted Christians: "Alleluia: for the Lord God omnipotent reigneth" (Rev. 19:6). Since He does and since He is still on His throne, it means for us a conquest of fear.

Franklin Roosevelt took office during the depression with the words, "We have nothing to fear but fear itself." That is even more true for the Christian. And surprisingly, all classes of people are beset with fears—fear of themselves, fear of others, fear of the present and the future, fear of sickness, of death, of poverty. There will never be a release from fear until we cease looking down instead of up. Robert Browning said, "Tis looking downward that mades one dizzy." Look up and find release from fear, for God reigns.

That God is still on His throne is also a comfort in our sorrow. Who among us has not felt at some time like Elijah—"I only am left." Be he wasn't and neither are we. Have we discovered that there is something higher in human experience than life's storms—the Lord God Himself?

We need to be reminded that the Bible is still the Word of God to men. Zedekiah asked Jeremiah, "Is there any word

70

from the Lord?" (37:17) and Jeremiah replied, "There is." Indeed there is, and the Bible is it. Because it is the authoritative Word from God, we have a guidebook for victorious living.

On a trip with another couple one day, we got lost. We had a map, and there was nothing wrong with it. We were just so busy with our conversation that we failed to consult the map. When we did study it we got back on the right highway. So it is with our life and the Word. When the way is lost, the Word will put us straight again.

In the Bible we have the prescription for true happiness. Eugene O'Neill, the playwright, once said: "If the human race is so stupid that in two thousand years it hasn't brains enough to appreciate that the secret of happiness is contained in one simple sentence . . . then it's time we dumped it down the nearest drain and let the ants have a chance. That simple sentence is 'For what shall it profit a man if he gain the whole world and lose his own soul.' "

We need to be reminded that the Savior is our refuge from an accusing conscience. Paul wrote, "There is therefore now no condemnation to them which are in Christ Jesus, who walk not after the flesh, but after the Spirit" (Rom. 8:1), and "Who shall lay any thing to the charge of God's elect? It is God that justifieth" (Rom. 8:33). We are delivered from our self-contempt because Jesus has set us free.

Yes, our memories often need to be prodded. We are prone to forget our deeds and our duties, our delights and our despair. When we look at the pit from where we came, who can help but praise God in all His works and ways!

Hymn: "The Rock that Is Higher"

29 BLESS YOU

Central Aim: To point out how tithing brings a blessing.

Prelude: "We Give Thee but Thine Own"

Call to Worship: "And all the tithe of the land, whether of the seed of the land, or of the fruit of the tree, is the Lord's: it is holy unto the Lord."—Lev. 27:30

Hymn: "All Things Are Thine"

Scripture: Malachi 3:10

Prayer: Make us generous of heart, O God, that we will give to Thee what is Thine and be good stewards of the blessing that remains.

MEDITATION

There are many provocative thoughts in this little passage. Here God offers a challenge: "bring all." How much of the tithe had His people been keeping for themselves? Had they perhaps been using the Lord's tithe like the woman who came in with her arms full of packages, saying to her husband, "I'm tired of keeping up with the Joneses. From now on they can keep up with me"? God offers a commitment: "I will open the windows of heaven." He opened those windows for Abraham and Jacob, for David and Daniel, and for Peter and Paul. God also offers a comfort: "I will pour you out a blessing." This blessing is conditioned on the tithe. Tithing is a recognition of God's power, a proof that you are depending on Him for everything.

Tithing will bless you by making you receptive to God's will. Our greatest privilege is the power to become a child of God. Our greatest bargain is to lose all things to win Christ. Our greatest profit is godliness in this life and the life yet to come. Our greatest inheritance is heaven and all its glories. Our greatest victory is to do God's will. Paul spoke of his fellow laborer, Epaphras, praying for the Colossians to "stand perfect and complete in all the will of God" (4:12). It is God's will that you are saved; are you? It is God's will that you grow in grace; do you? It is God's will that you are led of the Spirit; are you? It is God's will that you tithe; will you?

Tithing will bless you by lifting you to a higher plane of grace. It is a misconception to think of tithing as *giving* God the tenth. A few days ago I went into the bank, handed the cashier a check, and she gave me some currency. No—wait! Did she actually give me the money? No, she merely gave me what I had previously deposited. If I had had no money on deposit, she would not have cashed my check. It was my money to begin with. You cannot *give* God something that already belongs to Him. You are rightfully returning to Him His own.

Another misconception is that it is optional whether or not we tithe. I say this not from a legal viewpoint, nor a moral viewpoint, but from the very nature of God and faith. Is prayer optional? Is worship optional? Is personal witnessing optional? Is Bible reading optional? Is Christian living optional? Are missions optional? Not all Christians do these things, but by no means can it be said that God doesn't care whether or not we do. They are all means to greater grace in our lives.

Tithing will bless you in the birth of a more generous spirit. The natural thing is for us to be stingy and selfish. But the supernatural is for us to be free hearted and generous.

Abraham was unselfish with his land—and God used him.

Joseph was unselfish with his political power—and God used him.

Moses was unselfish with his spiritual power—and God used him.

Barnabas was unselfish with his possessions—and none has a fairer name in God's Book.

Tithing will bless you with a satisfied conscience. A man who loves his family is not embarrassed if the community should find out how much he spends on his loved ones. Why then should he turn red in the face if it should be discovered how much he gives to the family of God? He won't—unless it is so little that he feels little.

God did not say that tithing paid as insurance against disaster, misfortune, poverty, or pain. This "no" resounds from the ash heap where sits Job. This "no" echoes from Calvary where hangs the One who gave His all. But it does bless you with a satisfied conscience, with a joy of knowing and doing God's will, and a greater appreciation of God's material blessings—if and when He chooses to bestow them.

Hymn: "Trust, Try, and Prove Me"

30 NO WAY

Central Aim: To emphasize that Jesus is the only way of salvation.

Prelude: "The Old Rugged Cross"

Call to Worship: "Verily, verily, I say unto thee, Except a man be born again, he cannot see the kingdom of God."—John 3:3

Hymn: "There Is a Name I Love to Hear"

Scripture: Acts 4:12

Prayer: Open our hearts to rejoice anew at the salvation Thou hast provided through Jesus Christ, Thy Son and our Savior.

MEDITATION

The two young men were in an animated conversation. Suddenly, one exclaimed loudly enough to be overheard, "No way, man, no way." What was the topic—girls, cars, trips, politics? I'll never know. But if the subject was religion, that "no way, man, no way" might have been the doctrine of salvation. When Jesus said, "Ye must be born again," when Peter said, "Neither is there salvation in any other," they were saying: "No way, man, no way" to be saved except this way. For there is "none other name under heaven given among men, whereby we must be saved" (Acts 4:12).

We must be born again because we are sinners by nature, as well as sinners by choice and practice. We must be born again because God is holy, and holiness cannot abide with unholiness. But supremely we must be born again because Jesus said so. God's Son came from heaven to earth to be our Savior from sin, and He certainly knew what was necessary for our salvation. He who is wisdom incarnate would not be so foolish as to die for those who needed no sin offering to cover their guilt.

What a wealth of power there is in His name! When Peter healed the lame man at the Beautiful Gate of the Temple, the Sanhedrin questioned Peter and John asking, "By what power, or by what name, have ye done this?" (Acts 4:7). Peter replied, "By the name of Jesus Christ of Nazareth."

In His name is the forgiveness of sin. "To him give all the prophets witness, that through his name whosoever believeth in him shall receive remission of sins" (Acts 10:43). Sin is a drug to the soul, the instrument of everlasting ruin, the midnight of man's moral being. Its pleasures are poison and its revelry is ruin. Sin is a disease, a debt, and a departure. But in Jesus' name, the disease is healed, the debt is paid, and the departure is ended.

In His name is our salvation, our assurance in the face of death, our comfort in time of trouble, our strength in time of temptation, our help in the midst of the hazards of life.

He is an all-accessible Savior. By day or by night, here or across the world, He is ever ready, ever anxious to receive all who seek Him for the salvation of their soul.

He is an all-sufficient Savior. "Wherefore he is able also to save them to the uttermost that come unto God by him, seeing he ever liveth to make intercession for them" (Heb. 7:25). Jesus saves to the uttermost depths of depravity, to the uttermost degree of temptation, and to the uttermost duration of time or eternity. The vilest sinner or the weakest soul alike can receive His compassionate concern.

He is an everlasting Savior. No passing of the years can age Him, no passing of time can dim His radiance. He is a Savior never failing and never faltering.

He is the only Savior. Nothing else can compete, nothing else can compare with Jesus. He is the only way to the Father's house of glory.

Many individuals have put themselves forward as answers to man's problems. Many ways have been proposed as the solution for man's search for meaning and peace of soul. But Jesus said, "I am the way." Not *a way*—one of many—but *the way*. "No way, man, no way" to be satisfied except through Jesus.

Hymn: "Glory to His Name"

31 LSD

Central Aim: To explore Biblical principles that bear upon the use or nonuse of drugs

Prelude: "O Love that Wilt Not Let Me Go"

Call to Worship: "Keep thy heart with all diligence; for out of it are the issues of life."—Prov. 4:23

Hymn: "Just When I Need Him Most"

Scripture: Proverbs 16:2-3

Prayer: Lead us to so commit our ways to Thee, O Lord, that the temptations of those things that destroy body and mind will lose their power.

MEDITATION

In the midst of this turned-on and tuned-out generation, I am a firm believer in LSD. Not, let me hasten to add, of that type used by so many. Instead of the abbreviation for the acid, the LSD that I believe in stands for Let's Stop Drugs. Now, there is no directive in God's Word which imposes the command, "Thou shalt not consume addicting drugs." That does not mean, however, that the Bible has nothing to say relevant to the issue of drug use. The assessment of any issue involving human behavior must be examined in the light of broad Biblical principles in the absence of any specifics. What then are some of these principles that deal with this issue?

There is the principle of loyalty to God. "Thou shalt love the Lord thy God with all thine heart, and with all thy soul, and with all thy might" (Deut. 6:5). Jesus also said, "No man can serve two masters" (Matt. 6:24). But where is the addict's first loyalty? Above God, above family, above food, above honesty, above health, above a sound mind—the addict's first loyalty is to his habit.

There is the principle of glorifying God. Paul wrote to the Corinthians, "Whether therefore ye eat, or drink, or whatsoever ye do, do all to the glory of God" (I Cor. 10:31). Timothy Leary, the apostle of LSD, touted it as an aid to religious experience. Some of the tremendous truths revealed to those on a trip were written down by them to remember when they came down. Among them were: "I am an egotist," "God is everywhere," "Love is better than hate." Truth—but truth already revealed in the Bible. What drug use does is to obtain an escape from reality, but a real religious experience helps one to face reality.

There is the principle of bodily sanctity. Writing to the Corinthians, Paul said, "What? know ye not that your body is the temple of the Holy Ghost which is in you, which ye have of God, and ye are not your own? For ye are bought with a price: therefore glorify God in your body, and in your spirit, which are God's" (I Cor. 6:19-20). The drug addict is destroying both body and mind through the ever increasing craving. The alcoholic and the inveterate smoker find themselves in the same category. Dr. Herbert Spiegel, New York psychiatrist, has utilized the body sanctity concept to cure hard core smokers who want to quit. It is in the form of a three-point commitment that the patient repeats every one to two hours. It goes like this:

1. For my body, smoking is a poison.
2. I need my body to live.
3. I owe my body this respect and protection.

To be grateful to God for the body He has given you is a strong defense against destroying it.

There is the principle of sin's enslavement. "Know ye not, that to whom ye yield yourselves servants to obey, his servants ye are whom ye obey? whether of sin unto death, or of obedience unto righteousness?" (Rom. 6:16). We can choose our master; but once we have chosen, we must then obey. What a slave will do is absolutely determined by his master. Drug addiction is a cruel master to serve; and one that will drive his slave to lying, stealing, and murder.

There is the principle of individual influence. "For none of us liveth to himself" (Rom. 14:7). Seldom do people become addicts because they have decided to do so. They are introduced to some drug by a friend, who may also be a pusher. When they are hooked on it, they entice others in order to support their own habit and thereby become pushers. No person enters the stream of human history without either increasing or decreasing the sum total of human happiness. Everywhere a person will meet people who will be either better or worse for having met him.

The moral oughtness of the Bible is a master that excludes drug abuse on all counts.

Hymn: "Come, Thou Fount"

32 LIFE STYLE

Central Aim: To explore the life styles of people as set forth in the parables of Jesus.

Prelude: "A Charge to Keep Have I"

Call to Worship: "Commit thy way unto the Lord; trust also in him; and he shall bring it to pass."—Ps. 37:5

Hymn: "Give of Your Best"

Scripture: Luke 9:57-62

Prayer: Make us conscious, O God, of how we are living in comparison with how we ought to be living; and give us the strength to do something about it.

MEDITATION

"It's my life style," stormed the girl angrily as her parents tried to remonstrate with her. Values change, times change, conditions change. The sign of the times is a spiritual latitude as wide as the Sahara Desert and just as dry. Jesus was pointing out in this passage that one cannot determine his own life style and still be a committed disciple. Only one who is able to forget his own needs and wants, who is able to give God's kingdom precedence over every other loyalty is fit for the kingdom of God. A great many people reverence Christ, find a solemn authority in His teaching, and are moved at times to be really Christian. Yet they fail somehow to come to the point of any effective service. Jesus finds many joiners but few disciples.

The first man to come is the life style of a casual disciple. This is one to whom it is only an incident in his life to follow Jesus. He may be idealistic but he is also superficial. He is like one who has feet and heart stirred by the roll of drums and the march of feet but who has no intention of making long marches or fighting bloody battles.

What kind of life style do you have in relation to the Lord? Is it incidental or fundamental? Is it admiration or dedication? The casual disciple treats all things religious—prayer, church attendance, Bible study, righteous living—with a take-it-or-leave-it attitude. If it is receiving at the hand of the Lord, it fits his life style; if it is giving to the Lord, it does not.

The second man to come is the life style of convenience. A farmer cannot plow a field at just any old time. A businessman cannot open his business just as the notion strikes him and be successful. In the same way with discipleship, it is never safe to put off until tomorrow what should be done today. Do you put personal responsibilities before responsibilities to Christ? Do you ever find a convenient time to serve Christ?

80

A recent survey showed that 92 percent of families interviewed watched television together but only 17 percent worshiped together in the house of God. This man would serve—but later. The answer Jesus gave him has no harshness except in the sticky sentimentality of the worldly minded, who are great on flowers and words without meaning for the dead while they ignore the harsh reality of death without hope and without God.

The third man to come is the conditional life style. "I'll do this for you if you'll do that for me." How many there are who are more interested in using God than in being used by God. Do you want to be a disciple on your terms or God's? Do you think that you can serve Him just as you will and He will put His approval on it? Do you want to serve God in your way, or in His way?

Can you say like Jesus, "Not my will, but thine be done"?

Can you say like Mary, "Be it done unto me according to thy word"?

Can you say like John, "I must decrease, He must increase"?

Can you say like Paul, "What wilt thou have me to do, O Lord"?

There is another life style that is not presented. It is that of the committed disciple. He is the one who follows in faithfulness, in fellowship with the Lord at all times, and in fruitfulness of service.

"Lord, I will follow Thee, but. . . ." The decision is delayed, the life style is unchanged. If ever it is right to follow Jesus, it is right to follow Him now.

Hymn: "I'll Live for Him"

33 WHAT WILL I WEAR?

Central Aim: To secure a decision to live the Christian life to the best advantage for Jesus.

Prelude: "Give Me a Heart Like Thine"

Call to Worship: "And let us not be weary in well doing: for in due season we shall reap, if we faint not."—Gal. 6:9

Hymn: "Lift Me Up to Thee"

Scripture: Zechariah 3:3-4

Prayer: Lord, give us again the assurance that whatever our need, Thou hast already planned for its provision.

MEDITATION

How often have we asked the question, "But what will I wear?" We must wear something appropriate, but when we have worn a suit or dress many times we begin to feel that a different style or color is in order. The words *garment, cloak,* and *coat* are used in the Bible about two hundred times. We remember the covering of leaves made by Adam, the coat of many colors worn by Joseph, the purple robe that was put on the suffering Christ, His seamless robe for which the soldiers cast lots, the cloak that Paul had left in Troas and needed in Rome, the best robe that was brought forth for the Prodigal. Joshua was made to understand that he who stands in God's presence also has a certain wardrobe. Isaiah reminds us that "we are all as. . .filthy rags" (64:6). We can never enter into the presence of royalty robed in rags. We must discard the rags of sin and be attired in the garments of God. "What will I wear?" can be a question of eternal significance.

"What will I wear?"—wear the wedding garment. Jesus told of a wedding feast where every person present was supposed

to be robed in a garment furnished by the king. But when the king came to see the guests, there was a man present who was without the garment. This man was rejected and ejected from the premises.

"*What will I wear?*"—wear the robe of righteousness. Isaiah exulted, "I will greatly rejoice in the Lord, my soul shall be joyful in my God; for he hath clothed me with the garments of salvation, he hath covered me with the robe of righteousness" (61:10).

> *When He shall come with trumpet sound,*
> *Oh, may I then in Him be found,*
> *Dressed in His righteousness alone,*
> *Faultless to stand before the throne.*

"*What will I wear?*"—wear the cloak of humility. "Be clothed with humility: for God resisteth the proud, and giveth grace to the humble" (I Peter 5:5). Bernard of Clairvaux was fond of saying, "We are all humiliated but we do not all become humble." The experiences of life humiliate us; but instead of humbling some persons, they turn them into dispirited and discontented people, lowering their ideals and making them bitter, cynical, and discouraged. Humility confesses its sins and takes from the unmerited goodness of God; and so, like the child, is made happy again.

"*What will I wear?*"—wear the armor of God. "Put on the whole armour of God, that ye may be able to stand against the wiles of the devil" (Eph. 6:11). Paul tells us that this armor is the girdle of truth, the breastplate of righteousness, the shoes of the gospel, the shield of faith, the helmet of salvation, and the sword of the Spirit. This is not an outfit for retreat but for advance. One day we Christians are going to be discharged from the army of the Lord. In that day we will lay aside the armor of God and receive the white robe of the victorious in Jesus. "He that overcometh, the same shall be clothed in white raiment. . ." (Rev. 3:5).

Hymn: "O That Will Be Glory"

34 DON'T MENTION IT

Central Aim: To create the right motivation for giving.

Prelude: "Trust, Try, and Prove Me"

Call to Worship: "But seek ye first the kingdom of God, and his righteousness; and all these things shall be added unto you."—Matt. 6:33

Hymn: "Our Best"

Scripture: Matthew 6:1-4

Prayer: Lead us, Lord, to cherish the grace of giving. Teach us anew that it is not only the gift but also the spirit in which it is given that is important.

MEDITATION

Johnny had been invited by the next-door neighbor to go for a ride in his new automobile. When he returned he was unusually quiet. At the dinner table his mother asked him several questions about his afternoon, all of which he answered with a low, "Yes'm." Finally, his mother said, "Well, did you thank him?" Johnny replied in a low voice, "Yes'm. But he told me not to mention it." Have you ever been in the position of trying to thank someone for some good thing they have done for you or given you? As you try to stammer out your appreciation, they too may have said, "Don't mention it." But it does us good and warms their heart for us to mention it, and it does express our pleasure at their help or thoughtfulness. But they are correct in their attitude. It is as if they were saying, "I did not do it for praise. I did it because I wanted to."

Jesus warns us against the attitude of doing something simply to show off our generosity, win praise, and have the world say, "How good he is!" Why do you give? What is your underlying motive?

Some people give from motives of prestige. One of the French kings ceremoniously made out a gift deed of a whole province, dedicating it to the Virgin Mary. But he reserved the revenues of the province to the crown. As such, it was an empty gift.

The foundations which support TV programs for the raising of money know that all that is pledged will not come in. Some people call in simply because they want their name mentioned, along with the size of their gift. That is giving to the glory of self.

Jesus had a word to say about giving of this nature when He said, "They have their reward" (Matt. 6:2). Quite literally that is, "They have received their payment in full."

Some people give from a sense of duty. Knowing that they possess more than others do of this world's goods, they give because of a feeling that it is a duty they cannot very well escape. Yet sometimes the giving of money is what costs the least. A certain project was planned and a worker contacted a woman to secure her participation. Her answer was, "Whatever you do is fine with me. Let me know what it costs and I will give you a check." The worker quietly confided to another, "I'll be so glad when she learns that you cannot buy off from everything." Money must be given, to be sure. But time, trouble, service, and sympathy must also be given. If we give generously of things but never of self, the giving is incomplete.

Some people give because their heart will permit no other

answer. Such a person gives because he cannot rid himself of a sense of responsibility for the man in need. A compassionate heart will extend a helping hand.

One cold, wintry, rainy day, a friend of mine on his way into town passed a man who stood on the other side of the highway trying to thumb a ride in the opposite direction. My friend eyed the man, obviously cold with no coat, shoulders hunched against the slow rain. Continuing on until he found a place to turn, he drove back to the man. Hastily shrugging out of his jacket, he rolled down the window and thrust his jacket into the hands of the man. He then wheeled his car around and continued on his way. I asked him what led him to do that and he replied, "I can remember times like that." Surely such giving is from a grateful heart.

"Don't mention it" is advice we can apply to ourselves and our giving, both to God and to man.

Hymn: "Take My Life and Let It Be"

35 WOE IS ME

Central Aim: To show the way to turn the disappointments of life into spiritual victories.

Prelude: "His Way with Thee"

Call to Worship: "If ye then be risen with Christ, seek those things which are above, where Christ sitteth on the right hand of God."—Col. 3:1

Hymn: "I Must Tell Jesus"

Scripture: Jeremiah 10:19

Prayer: Dear God, lead us to so trust Thee that in the times of feeling overwhelmed we will know that we truly are not.

MEDITATION

"Woe" is an exclamation found in both Hebrew and Greek to denote hurt, pain, sorrow, or grief. It is widely used in the Bible but not so often heard today. However, probably nothing could be more expressive of our feeling in times of stress than Jeremiah's lament, "Woe is me." Shakespeare put these words in Ophelia's mouth after her encounter with Hamlet in which he pretended madness:

> *O woe is me,*
> *To have seen what I have seen, see what I see.*

Shelley captured its essence in "Adonais" when he wrote:

> *Ah, woe is me! Winter is come and gone,*
> *But grief returns with the revolving year.*

"Woe is me" is a feeling to which we are subject—but for what reason? Is it trivial or traumatic? Will it tender or toughen our character?

Do we feel woe because of our companions and place of dwelling? The psalmist did. "Woe is me, that I sojourn in Mesech, that I dwell in the tents of Kedar!" (120:5). He may not literally have lived in such places, but he at least dwelt among people to whom the comparison was a likeness. Why did he dwell there? Did his business, or trade, or livelihood demand it? Or was it by his own choice? Lot dwelt in Sodom by his own choice, even though it vexed his righteous soul. Many Israelites remained in Babylon by choice, even when they were free to return to Jerusalem. Whatever the reason, a person can hardly be subjected to a greater trial than to be mixed in a society with which he has no sympathy and which has so sympathy with him.

Do we feel woe because of our discontentment? Baruch did. "Thus saith the Lord, the God of Israel, unto thee, O Baruch; Thou didst say, Woe is me now! for the Lord hath added grief to my sorrow; I fainted in my sighing, and I find no rest" (Jer. 45:2-3). What was wrong with Baruch? Three things: (1) a prominent self-concern that he was to suffer— "woe is *me* now"; (2) a murmuring spirit against God—"the Lord hath *added* grief"; and (3) a fretful despondency—"I find *no* rest." Instead of hiding in God's care and love amid distress, Baruch despaired. In the crisis he forgot the comfort.

Do we feel woe because we are misunderstood? Jeremiah did. "Woe is me, my mother, that thou hast borne me a man of strife and a man of contention to the whole earth!" (15:10). Because Jeremiah's contemporaries never heard his prayers on their behalf or knew the burden of his spirit for them, they judged him to be a contentious, fault-finding, critical individual. No man ever longed to be called a man of peace more than Jeremiah, but his call made him appear as a man of strife. Again, it was so for three reasons:

1. He did not comply with popular sins. Elijah, John the Baptist, and Jesus all spoke against sin and were all considered men of strife.

2. He was in advance of his time. It is said that nothing is more powerful than a truth whose time has come. But the pioneers of progress who are seeking to give that truth its birth are not often well received.

3. He was in earnest. A spirit true to God cannot agree to just leave things alone and let every man go his own way.

"Woe is me"—when? When I know the will of God and do

it not. When I know the love of God and spread it not. When I know the care of God and share it not. When I know the riches of God and have not my portion.

Hymn: "He Keeps Me Singing"

36 APPEARANCES ARE DECEIVING

Central Aim: To point out that God's measurements are often different from our own.

Prelude: "Praise Him, Praise Him"

Call to Worship: "The Lord is righteous in all his ways, and holy in all his works."—Ps. 145:17

Hymn: "Standing on the Promises"

Scripture: I Samuel 16:7

Prayer: Remind us, dear God, that we do not have Thy knowledge and cannot judge the heart and intent as Thou canst. Keep us from the snap judgments that are so often wrong.

MEDITATION

My wife has a bowl of artificial fruit which rested for some time on a coffee table. On several pieces, perfect little teeth marks give mute evidence that their appearance was deceiving to some child. In the same manner, human judgments about people are almost always superficial. The relaxed and easy manner, the suave gestures, and the polished glitter have often led men—and women—astray. Many notable figures of history who were once headliners have now shrunk to a mere footnote.

Jesus warned His listeners, "Judge not according to the appearance, but judge righteous judgment" (John 7:24). Muscularity is not Christianity and the body beautiful is not holiness. While the body is to be a matter of care and concern, it is not how we look but rather what we are that is most important. A selfish disposition, a sordid soul, or a sinful life coupled with outside beauty is like a "jewel in a swine's snout."

Appearances are often deceiving where people are concerned. Samuel still had in his mind's eye the sight of King Saul who stood "higher than any of the people from his shoulders and upward." Of him, Samuel said, "There is none like him among all the people" (I Sam. 10:23-24). But Samuel could not see the hasty, rash, disobedient nature that never learned to humble itself before God.

Of Absalom it is written, "But in all Israel there was none to be so much praised as Absalom for his beauty: from the sole of his foot even to the crown of his head there was no blemish in him" (II Sam. 14:25). All in all, Absalom might have sat as the subject for Shakespeare when he wrote: "What a piece of work is man! how noble in reason! how infinite in faculty! in form and moving how express and admirable! in action how like an angel! in apprehension how like a god! the beauty of the world! the paragon of animals!" And Absalom cunningly disguised his inner nature until he had stolen the hearts of Israel and nearly stolen the throne from his father, David.

Appearances are often deceiving where events are concerned. On a cold morning in February of 1809, two neighbors met on a mountain ridge. "Anything new?" asked one. "Nothing much, except Tom and Nancy had a baby. Named him Abe," replied the other. How were they to know what God had invested in Abraham Lincoln?

The loss of a citizen and his family meant nothing to mighty Ur of the Chaldees, but it marked the beginning of God's chosen people.

Pharaoh probably thought, "A good riddance" when Moses fled to Horeb; but God was making Moses familiar with the passageway of the Israelites.

A famine in Moab seemed no different from any other, but it led to Ruth the Gentile becoming an ancestress of the Lord.

An arrow aimed at nothing left the bow of a soldier, but it pierced Ahab and brought to pass the prophecy of Elijah.

Jehoiakim cut the scroll of God with a knife and then burned it, thinking he had destroyed it. But Jehoiakim is long dead, and the Word of God lives on.

Let us beware of being deceived by appearances lest the mirage cheat us out of the reality.

Hymn: "Trusting Jesus, That Is All"

37 COPYCAT

Central Aim: To lead Christians to create more of the likeness of Christ in their daily walk and talk.

Prelude: "My Jesus, I Love Thee"

Call to Worship: "See that none render evil for evil unto any man; but ever follow that which is good, both among yourselves, and to all men."—I Thess. 5:15

Hymn: "Footsteps of Jesus"

Scripture: I Corinthians 11:1

Prayer: Dear Lord, cleanse our hearts of our foolish pride and will that we may have more of Thy Spirit and be able to walk in the ways of Jesus forever.

MEDITATION

"Copycat, copycat" is a taunt of derision cried by children of every generation. And to a great extent it is true of us all. It is true because human behavior is determined more by the power of personal example than by all the promises of religion, all the writings of moralists, all the warnings of psychologists, or all the theories of educators combined. Imitation of those on whom we depend, admire, love, or envy is well-nigh irresistible. Because this is true, it is proper for us to be highly selective in choosing someone for our pattern.

The word *followers* is derived from the same word from which we get our English word *mimic,* and it means "imitator." Paul uses this word in I Corinthians 4:16 where he says, "Wherefore I beseech you, be ye imitators of me." He uses it in I Thessalonians 1:6 where he says, "And ye became imitators of us and of the Lord, having received the word in much affliction, with joy of the Holy Spirit." We are called to imitate the apostles, but only insofar as they imitated Christ. "I have given you an example," said Jesus (John 13:15). And we are to be imitators of that example.

We should be imitators of the love of Jesus. That love is never mere emotionalism, but is always a real and practical thing. The portrait of love is drawn in I Corinthians 13 and the model for that portrait is plainly Jesus. It shows us that Christlikeness is love expressed in terms of relationships. Love is revealed in the performance of service.

Love is service that is unlimited: "all things whatsoever ye would that men should do to you, do ye even so to them" (Matt. 7:12). Whatever is good, profitable, just, or pleasant for yourself—by that judge your neighbor's need. Love is service that ranges beyond our circles. We all draw circles. The egotist draws a very small one. The Lord drew a great big one that included the sinner and the hopeless along with the upright and faithful.

> *He drew a circle that shut me out—*
> *Heretic, rebel, a thing to flout.*
> *But love and I had the wit to win:*
> *We drew a circle that took him in.*
>
> Edwin Markham

How big is your circle?

We should be imitators in cross bearing. So much of the religion of today is a reflection of our culture, not a reflection of our Christ. So many feel no necessity of a cross; they want only buttons to be pushed. They want the approach which says, "Think right and be successful," or "How to pray all your tensions away." Certainly we are not called on to shoulder anything like "the old rugged cross," but there are crosses for us. How about the cross of concern for a broken and bleeding world in sin and want? How about the cross of concern for the social order in which we live?

We should be imitators in loving obedience. An undivided loyalty to God was expressed in the words, "My meat is to do the will of him that sent me" (John 4:34). That is the one claim to which all others must be subjected. As imitators of Christ we ought also to have the sense of an absolute dependence on God. Jesus posed for us the parable of two sons to teach us the principles. On which son would you rather pattern your life—the son who said, "I will go" but never did, or the son who said no but then did do his father's will?

93

Jesus has not only given us an absolutely perfect pattern, He also constantly helps us to follow it.

Hymn: "I'll Live for Him"

38 WAIT A MINUTE

Central Aim: To point out the importance of a prompt response to the claims of Christ.

Prelude: "Why Do You Wait?"

Call to Worship: "Walk in wisdom toward them that are without, redeeming the time."—Col. 4:5

Hymn: "To the Work"

Scripture: II Corinthians 6:2

Prayer: Teach us to so number our days and guard our time that when the end comes we will not be ashamed of our work for Jesus.

MEDITATION

Who among us has not at some time either answered, or had answered, a request by the words "wait a minute." How often those words are used as a delaying tactic in the face of some duty or chore we do not want to perform! "Procrastination," said Edward Young, "is the thief of time." Donald Marquis may have been a little kinder when he said that "procrastination is the art of keeping up with yesterday." When we use these words, we are easing our conscience by not making it a deliberate refusal, and easing it more by naming a ridiculously short period of time. If we are going to do it in a minute, we might just as well go ahead immediately. What we are really saying is that we intend to do it—but not right now.

This is true of salvation. Few, if any, set out to deliberately go to hell. But traveling "the road of by and by" leads to "the land of never." This is why the Bible says, "Behold, now is the accepted time. . ." (II Cor. 6:2).

"Wait a minute" is often our answer to God's call to service. When one disciple said that he must first go bury his father, and another wished to first bid farewell to his family before following Jesus, they were saying in essence "wait a minute." And as Christ calls us today to serve Him, we frequently respond with "wait a minute."

Perhaps this attitude has never been captured any better than in this poem whose author is unknown but which is often credited to the Negro poet Paul Laurence Dunbar.

The Lord had a job for me, but I had so much to do,
I said, "You get somebody else—or wait till I get through."
I don't know how the Lord came out, but He seemed to get along,
But I felt kind o'sneakin' like—knowed I'd done God wrong.

One day I needed the Lord, needed Him right away—
And He never answered me at all, but I could hear him say,
Down in my accusin' heart—"Nigger, I'se got too much to do.
You get somebody else or wait till I get through."

Now when the Lord has a job for me, I never tries to shirk;

I drops what I have on hand and does the good
Lord's work;
And my affairs can run along, or wait till I get
through.
Nobody else can do the work that God's marked
out for you.

We all want to be more like Jesus, but not right now or not
too fast. We want to grow in grace, but not too quickly.
Moses had that problem. "Wait a minute, Lord, I'm not the
man you want." How we are prone to back away!

The reminder we need is that the key word of the Bible is
not "wait a minute" but "now."

Hymn: "Trust and Obey"

39 SORRY ABOUT THAT

Central Aim: To secure the right spirit of repentance.

Prelude: "Back to Bethel"

Call to Worship: "The Lord is not slack concerning his
promise, as some men count slackness; but is longsuffering to usward, not willing that any should perish, but
that all should come to repentance."—II Peter 3:9

Hymn: "I Am Resolved"

Scripture: Luke 13:3

Prayer: Lead us, O God, to the contrite spirit and broken
heart that Thou wilt not refuse, and to the path of
righteousness for Jesus' sake.

MEDITATION

There is a certain character in a television program who excuses his errors with a glib, "Sorry about that." Now, it is very easy to say "I'm sorry" or "Sorry about that"; but for a real repentance there must be more than a surface conviction. Pharaoh had a repentance that cried, "Take away the frogs," and David had a repentance that cried, "Take away my sin." Perhaps one reason for the popularity of the phrase "Sorry about that" is that deep down in the human heart lies buried the feeling that there is a need for repentance. The times in which we live cry out for repentance. There is a false sense of security resting on the twin idols of scientific advance and economic prosperity. There is a constant expansion of crime and a constant decline of the morals of our nation.

Is there no balm in all Gilead? Yes, there is a balm in Gilead; but we are stricken, smitten with the sores of sin because there is no real turning to God in repentance. Real repentance is a particular experience that produces a permanent impression. As Paul pointed out, "Godly sorrow worketh repentance to salvation not to be repented of: but the sorrow of the world worketh death" (II Cor. 7:10).

To be really "sorry about that" is a process. Repentance passes through certain well-defined stages. It is not a matter of tears, nor the ideas of good intentions. It is a personal response that demands:

1. A conviction—"And when he is come, he will reprove the world of sin and of righteousness, and of judgment" (John 16:8).

2. A contrition—"The sacrifices of God are a broken spirit: a broken and a contrite heart, O God, thou wilt not despise" (Ps. 51:17).

3. A confession—"For I acknowledge my transgressions: and my sin is ever before me. Against thee, thee only, have I sinned, and done this evil in thy sight" (Ps. 51:3-4).

97

4. A conversion—"And the children of Israel said unto the Lord, we have sinned: do thou unto us whatsoever seemeth good unto thee: deliver us only, we pray thee, this day. And they put away the strange gods from among them and served the Lord" (Judg. 10:15-16).

5. A consecration—"But showed first unto them of Damascus, and at Jerusalem, and throughout all the coasts of Judea, and then to the Gentiles, that they should repent and turn to God, and do works meet for repentance" (Acts 26:20).

To really be "sorry about that" calls for a commitment. It calls for an intellectual commitment that means a change of view, such as David asked for: "Purge me with hyssop and I shall be clean: wash me, and I shall be whiter than snow" (Ps. 51:7). It calls for an emotional commitment that means a change of feeling, such as David desired: "Create in me a clean heart, O God; and renew a right spirit within me" (Ps. 51:10). It calls for a volitional commitment that means a change of purpose. Sin has corrupted the original purpose of our lives, and we must exercise the will to revert back from sin to serving God.

To be really "sorry about that" is to take an opportunity granted by God. "Then hath God also to the Gentiles granted repentance unto life" (Acts 11:18). That is an opportunity urged on us by the consequence of sin, by the goodness of God, and by the admonitions of the Old Testament prophets and the New Testament apostles.

Hymn: "The Way of the Cross"

40 HEARTBURN

Central Aim: To revive hearts that have grown gray and cold.

Prelude: "Pentecostal Power"

Call to Worship: "Wilt thou not revive us again: that thy people may rejoice in thee?"—Ps. 85:6

Hymn: "Revive Us Again"

Scripture: Luke 24:32-35

Prayer: Dear Lord, revive us now that we may return to the fire of our first love without any further delay.

MEDITATION

From the number of preparations extolled in the market place, I would say that Americans must suffer tremendously from heartburn. With the sound of a siren in the background we are urged to put out the fire by using Preparation X. It may well be necessary for us to use such preparations from time to time to put down heartburn due to acid indigestion, excessive eating, or tension. But the thing we need least of all is something to put out the heartburn caused by close communion with Christ. Christ may not appear in visible form to us, but the infallible sign that we are in fellowship with Him is that our hearts are spiritually warm.

The burning heart for Jesus is our greatest need. It should be a heart hot with love for Christ. John Wesley wrote of his Aldersgate experience, "About a quarter before nine, while he was describing the change which God works in the heart through faith in Christ, I felt my heart strangely warmed."

Gipsy Smith said, "The secret of whatever success God has given me is not in my head, it is in my heart."

It should be a heart hot with love for souls. Listen to Paul,

99

"For I could wish that myself were accursed from Christ for my brethren, my kinsmen according to the flesh" (Rom. 9:3); "My heart's desire and prayer to God for Israel is, that they might be saved" (Rom. 10:1); "Remember that by the space of three years I ceased not to warn every one night and day with tears" (Acts 20:31).

We need a heart hot with love for things of eternal value: a hot heart for a clear conscience, a hot heart for a deathless life, a hot heart for inward spiritual power and outward physical performance.

But the burning heart can be quenched. It is quenched by unconfessed sin. When we sin, it is because we take our eyes from the Lord; because we quit reading His Word; and because we grieve the Holy Spirit until He becomes silent and no longer rebukes us. Does God seem far away to you? Could the reason be found in Isaiah, "But your iniquities have separated between you and your God, and your sins have hid his face from you, that he will not hear" (59:2)? Have you justified yourself in what you are doing? "There is a way which seemeth right unto a man, but the end thereof are the ways of death" (Prov. 14:12).

But all is not lost! The burning heart can be rekindled. It can be set to flaming by the reading of the Word. For the instruction of these disciples, Jesus began at the beginning— the writings of Moses—and showed them through all the Scripture of the Old Testament how it pointed to Him.

The burning heart can also be rekindled by confessing our sin and need. The promise is secure: "If we confess our sins, he is faithful and just to forgive us our sins, and to cleanse us from all unrighteousness" (I John 1:9). This is really coming to grips with the issue. "Lord, I have sinned" is good for a starter—but face your sin. "Lord, I lost my temper." "Lord, I have lied." "Lord, I have stolen." Then He will answer and heal.

Nothing will ever be too hard to try, nothing will ever be too hard to bear, if we can only say as did these disciples, "Did not our heart burn within us while he talked with us?" (Luke 24:32).

Hymn: "Lord, Send a Revival"

41 BEGGARS CAN'T BE CHOOSERS

Central Aim: To foster the spirit of gratitude toward God.

Prelude: "Now Thank We All Our God"

Call to Worship: "Enter into his gates with thanksgiving and into his courts with praise: be thankful unto him, and bless his name."—Ps. 100:4

Hymn: "Count Your Blessings"

Scripture: Acts 3:1-10

Prayer: Lord, we beseech Thee to make us grateful for the blessings we receive from Thy hand. Remind us that all we have or hope to be comes from Thee.

MEDITATION

It happened during the thirties when money was scarce. The mother was on her way to town to do some necessary shopping when she turned to her daughter asking, "Elaine, what do you want me to bring you—a purse or some socks?" Elaine replied, "I'll be so glad when I don't have to buy something I need." But when there is no other choice, beggars can't be choosers.

It was fortunate for the man at the Beautiful Gate that he

could not be a chooser. He was expecting a handout of some amount from Peter. Had he his choice, he probably would have taken this rather than the unknown of what Peter had to offer. But he was a beggar, a man whose heart beat but whose feet refused to bear him up. How many years he had spent in this spot we are not told. No doubt he knew all the details of the worship service going on within the temple. He may even have known some of those who went in and out of the temple. But he remained on the outside, begging in hopes of a touched heart throwing something his way. On this day he got more than he would even have thought to ask for. We likewise are shameless beggars for God's grace, and neither can we be choosers about it.

Beggars can't be choosers when they are without strength. And we are without strength when we are unsaved. We are in nothing but rags before God—but He gives us redemption untold. We have nothing but a beggarly poverty—but He gives us riches better than gold. There is an old song that expresses those riches:

> I'd rather be a beggar,
> Live in a little shack by the road,
> Than to own all earth's treasures,
> With no title to a heavenly abode.

We have nothing but misery—but He gives us mercy; we have nothing but shame—but He gives us showers of blessings. A hive of bees can take a common worker bee and change it into a queen bee by feeding it a certain kind of diet. But it takes more than a diet to change man's moral nature, it takes the grace of God. And this is what God did for us when we were yet weak beggars. "For when we were yet without strength, in due time Christ died for the ungodly" (Rom. 5:6).

We may even be without strength when we are saved.

Some Christians appear to be lame from their new birth. God does not require of us that we be rich or learned or influential. He does not require that we be successful as the world counts success. He does not even expect of us that we perform miracles or work signs and wonders. But it is required of every Christian that he *be* a miracle, a miracle of God's redeeming grace—a man or a woman whom the world cannot explain because they do not know the mold from which he has been cut.

Beggars can't be choosers with what God has given. Suppose this man had not gone into the temple but instead went at once to inspect another building of which he had heard, but never seen. Would we not think of him as showing a base ingratitude? Isn't it strange that so many people want the gifts of God without the church of God? They seek to put themselves in the strange position of an alien: one who enjoys all the pleasures and most of the privileges of a country without becoming a citizen with his corresponding responsibilities.

We simply cannot choose to give God the fragments of our time and talents or the crumbs of consecration. We have no choice but to be committed to Him like Borden of Yale, "without reservation, without regret, and without retreat."

Hymn: "Serve the Lord with Gladness"

42 ALL FOR THE BEST

Central Aim: To explore the problem of pain and suffering.

Prelude: "Abide with Me"

Call to Worship: "Comfort ye, comfort ye my people, saith your God."—Isa. 40:1

Hymn: "Does Jesus Care?"

Scripture: Romans 8:28

Prayer: O God of all comfort, we have drunk deep at the well of Thy comfort in our tribulation, and beseech that Thou shouldest use us therefore to comfort others in their troubles.

MEDITATION

"Pain and pleasure, like light and darkness, succeed each other." But it is extremely difficult to convince someone who is suffering physical or mental pain that all is for the best. On the tongues of some people that statement is only a glib phrase intended to cheer and console. On the tongues of others it is a certainty born in the crucible of experience. Pain is no problem to the unbeliever. He can accept his pain without having to justify his God. But for one who believes in the presence, power, and love of God, it does pose a problem. Part of the problem lies in our own nature. We want automobiles fast enough to provide needed transportation, but we deplore the deaths caused by speed. We want knives sharp enough to cut, but not our fingers. We want water we can swim in, but not drown in. We want fire to warm the house, but not to burn the children. Pain is a part of life that we cannot evade. Since it is built into the world in which we live, how can it be that it is all for the best?

Pain is all for the best because it is a monitor of our health. Some years ago, I had a nagging pain in my side. It was never too sharp, but it never disappeared. Finally, I went to the doctor, then to the hospital, and had a diseased appendix removed. Had it not caused me pain, that appendix could have burst before I knew that I was ill. Pain warned me of the danger, and may even have saved my life.

Pain is all for the best because we cannot have all the assets of life and refuse its liabilities. There are two laws which operate at this point: the law of retribution for moral evil and the law of the uniformity of nature. Is it not only too true that the pains of war, famine, and pestilence are often caused by human selfishness? Floods have often occurred as the result of an irresponsible policy followed by the lumber industry, in which they took away from the hills their natural means of holding back rainwater. Epidemics may be caused by overcrowding in unsanitary conditions as the result of lust for financial gain without regard to human cost. Accidents are often caused by human thoughtlessness and selfishness. But we cannot do away with the lumber company, the landlords, or people.

On the other hand, nature works according to regular laws. These laws are necessary to provide us with a stable environment. Sometimes it would be vastly to our advantage if these laws would bend and let us dodge them. For example, how nice it would be when we trip and fall if the sidewalk would become as soft as grass. But these laws will not bend, and pain is the price we pay to avoid the terrifying alternative of having nothing fixed in the universe. In providing that stable environment for us, nature must also decree that not all situations are equally agreeable to all persons. The farmer may be well pleased to see the rain on his field while the bride is in dismay because her garden wedding is ruined.

Pain is all for the best because a safe and easy world does not provide a favorable condition for our mental, moral, spiritual, and social development. Genial climates do not always produce the best type of man. Often a person in a struggle against pain and disease emerges with traits and characteristics unknown to his personality before his ordeal. It frequently turns out that what happens *to* us is not nearly so important as what happens *in* us. When pain—physical or spiritual—comes, will our attitude be one of rebellion and anger, or will we accommodate ourselves to this intrusion into our lives and come to peace with it?

Pain is all for the best because it can teach us humility. We become so busy looking at ourselves that we forget to look at God. Then the pain comes and we remember God. This is no new discovery. David experienced it long ago and said, "It is good for me that I have been afflicted, that I might learn thy statutes" (Ps. 119:71). Someone has observed that the only time some people look up to God is when they are flat on their backs in a sickbed.

Hymn: "Just When I Need Him Most"

43 DON'T BE A LITTERBUG

Central Aim: To develop an awareness of a Christian's need to show the better example.

Prelude: "Follow On"

Call to Worship: "And have no fellowship with the unfruitful works of darkness, but rather reprove them."—Eph. 5:11

Hymn: "Our Best"

Scripture: Philippians 3:13-14

Prayer: Lead us, O loving Father, to an understanding of our influence on others. Protect us from being the cause of someone else's stumbling.

MEDITATION

On almost any highway, you will see the sign "Don't be a litterbug." Other signs might tell you that the fine for littering ranges from ten to two hundred dollars. Litterbags are provided by some service stations and litter barrels are conveniently placed by the highway departments. All of this is an effort to save on the millions of dollars spent each year cleaning up after the American public. America is on the move; and everywhere she goes there is a trail of wrappers, sacks, cartons, bottles, and cans.

"Don't be a litterbug" is good advice for keeping America beautiful and good advice for keeping Christians spiritually healthy. Paul's life was one of thrilling spiritual progress. He simply refused to litter life's highway with a lot of trash. And so should we.

Let us not litter life's highway with bad influences. Up in Pennsylvania is a beautiful wooded park. At the entrance hangs this sign:

> *Let no one say—and say it to your shame—*
> *That all was beauty here until you came.*

That can be applied to life also:

Was all at peace and harmony until you came into the family, or church, or club, or on the job?

Was some individual making progress in the way of righteousness when you became the stumbling block? The most striking funeral sentence I can remember was delivered at the service of a young man who died an alcoholic. Very simply it was: "His best friends were his worst enemies."

Was a fine relationship being built until you tossed off a foolish and impulsive remark? "I just didn't think," we say; but the damage is done. Our thoughtlessness can litter life with bad influences.

Let us not litter life's highway with broken vows. We are reminded that "Better is it that thou shouldest not vow, than that thou shouldest vow and not pay" (Eccles. 5:5).

The divorce courts are littered with the shattered pieces of broken vows—broken usually by selfishness. The church rolls are padded with the names of individuals who conveniently forgot their vows to God. Every organization has those who accept leadership positions and then forget their vows to faithful service.

It was Dietrich Bonhoeffer who popularized the phrase "cheap grace." Bonhoeffer preached against the Nazi evil until he was put to death. "Cheap grace" is the desire to have all God's blessings without any cost. "Cheap grace" is causing life's highway to be littered with broken vows.

Let us not litter life's highway with cast-off responsibilities. There is such a thing as returning the kindness shown to us. Oh, perhaps not to the one who did it for us, but for someone else who is now in the place where we once were. Have we ever returned the flowers sent when we were ill, the letters that encourage, the visits that rejoice, or the hand that was extended to help in a time of trouble? Lord Byron was right when he wrote:

> *All who joy would win,*
> *Must share it—happiness was born a twin.*

Don't be a litterbug with your life. Let it be clean and pure without and within by the grace of God. If our lives are full of litter or trash, let it be burned up by the Spirit of fire from our God. And let us not bear but rather praise Him that He is a consuming fire. As such He can sweep through our lives like a torch and leave our highway of life free from such unsightly litter.

Hymn: "I Would Be True"

44 WOULD YOU BELIEVE

Central Aim: To point out the folly in the neglect of salvation.

Prelude: "He Included Me"

Call to Worship: "How shall we escape, if we neglect so great salvation; which at the first began to be spoken by the Lord, and was confirmed unto us by them that heard him."—Heb. 2:3

Hymn: "Redeemed, How I Love to Proclaim It"

Scripture: Jeremiah 2:12

Prayer: Heavenly Father, we thank Thee and praise Thee for the gift of salvation. Help us to give all our heart to Jesus in gratitude for His death on our behalf.

MEDITATION

A certain television program has greatly popularized the phrase "Would you believe?" A few days ago I was. in a drive-in grocery when I overheard two boys who appeared to be about nine or ten years of age. One asked the other, "How much was it?" The other replied, "Would you believe a hundred dollars?"

Jeremiah uses strong terms to indicate the amazement of the holy ones in heaven at the monstrous folly of human sin. The inhabitants of the earth could have God for their friend, but they have chosen Him for their enemy. This indeed is cause for astonishment. There are some things that prevail today—nearly two thousand years after God has come in Christ to reveal Himself—that are hard for us to believe.

Would you believe that so many allow themselves to be deceived as to the way of salvation? There is only one way. "Neither is there salvation in any other: for there is none other name under heaven given among men, whereby we must be saved" (Acts 4:12). The question is not whether we are Buddhists, or Baptists, Catholics, or Protestants; the question is our identity with Christ.

Philosophies, prophecies, angels, saints, council, creeds, and connections shall all fail; but Jesus will never fail. For His is the name above all names, and there is no other.

Would you believe that men would take such fearful risks regarding the future? "How shall we escape if we neglect so great salvation?" (Heb. 2:3). That is a question that neither an angel above nor a devil below can answer. To neglect salvation surely is:

To be guilty of immeasurable folly.

To be guilty of an appalling presumption on God's grace.

To be guilty of the most base ingratitude.

To be guilty of contemptuous defiance.

Would you believe that men could remain so unconcerned while living in this evil age? On the right hand and on the left the ravages of sin are apparent. Sin degrades our youth and demoralizes our old. Sin destroys our politics, disgraces our economics, and debases our society. It robs us of virtue, ruins our purity, and wrecks our righteousness. It fills the hospitals, the penitentiaries, and the cemeteries.

Its pleasures are sweet, its promises are rosy, and its end is death. Isaiah said, "Our iniquities, like the wind, have taken us away" (64:6). Sin took Adam from the beautiful garden of God; it took Jacob from the tents of Isaac; it took Israel from the Promised Land into captivity; it took Jonah from the path of duty; it took David from the ways of righteousness; it took Demas from the course of duty; and it took Ananias from the land of the living. The woe of sin in this world ought to stir every heart to concern.

Would you believe that men would treat the Savior with the disrespect that they do? Yet they do, ignoring the fact that "by his own blood he . . . obtained eternal redemption for us" (Heb. 9:12). He suffered the wages of sin, which He did not earn, that we might receive eternal life, which we do not deserve. And as long as earth stands we will have cause to be astonished at what man does in the light of God's goodness.

Hymn: "Are You Washed in the Blood?"

45 AS FAR AS I CAN SEE

Central Aim: To reflect on the providence of God in His world.

Prelude: "This Is My Father's World"

Call to Worship: "I had fainted, unless I had believed to see the goodness of the Lord in the land of the living."—Ps. 27:13

Hymn: "God Moves in a Mysterious Way"

Scripture: I Corinthians 13:12

Prayer: O God, we confess that we are but children stumbling in the dark when it comes to Thy ways. But we commit ourselves to Thee because of Thy care for us.

MEDITATION

There is a phrase we often use to confess that we do not know what is in the present or the future, or when we are in doubt or perplexity about something. That phrase is "As far as I can see." How far can we see? Is it not true that many times we are puzzled by what we see? That as far as logic or reason is concerned a certain thing should be true, but somehow just isn't?

The Bible reflects the grace of God, but have we not at many times and in many circumstances cried out to God because we did not understand what was taking place in our lives? The Bible reflects the love of God, but is it not difficult for us to see His love in the heartbreak of divorce or disaster or death? There are some things we must say about our ability to see or not to see.

To be sure, God's purpose is often contained in the unseen. Faith is the assurance of our hopes that makes us certain of realities which we do not see.

Sight saw only a baby boy being brought to the temple at the proper time, but faith saw salvation and the long awaited Messiah. Only Simeon was able to say, "Lord, now lettest thou thy servant depart in peace, according to thy word: For mine eyes have seen thy salvation" (Luke 2:29-30).

Sight saw only a rough fisherman, temperamental and variable, but faith saw a stalwart defender of the faith, immovable and abounding in the work of the Lord.

Sight saw only two mites being dropped into the temple collection, but faith saw the abounding love that gave out of poverty with nothing to spare.

Sight saw only the carpenter from Nazareth; but faith saw the Master Builder, without whom nothing was created.

112

Sight saw only a rough wooden cross with a man hanging on it, but faith saw the eternal love of God wherein Christ died for us while we were yet sinners.

To be sure, our evaluation of all others must also consider the unseen. In all our human relationships there are things not seen for which we must look. Have you ever taken a stroll on a moonlit night? If so, you know that in the reflected light of the moon everything is indistinct, standing half-revealed and half-concealed. So it is with life.

Take, for example, the motivation that is behind someone's deeds. How much do we really know about those motives? We may dimly understand; but unless we have lived that life, known all its influences and environment, we could not know perfectly its motives. Or consider a person's inner resources. How well do we know that? Does he have deep wells within which will sustain him in the parched periods of life? How much can he take before he cracks? The disappointments, the unseen sacrifices, and the unknown deeds of thoughtfulness for others are only partially seen by us.

What do you see when you look on others? For what you see is determined to a large extent by what you are.

The men who brought the woman and flung her at the feet of Jesus did not see a person to be pitied and restored. They saw only a person taken in adultery—for so they were.

The Pharisee who stood in the temple and prayed, thanking God that he was not an extortioner like the publican, could not see that in one manner or another he likewise was an extortioner.

The men who hotly accused the disciples did not see in them brothers. They saw only Sabbath-breakers—for so they were.

God Himself looks beyond our sins, our faults, our glaring weaknesses to see the possibilities and qualities which give promise of what we can be instead of dwelling on what we presently are. Thus our own development is in the unseen.

113

Paul tells us that the things we see are transitory but the things we do not see are eternal.

> *Only faintly now I see Him*
> *With the darkling veil between*
> *But a blessed day is coming,*
> *When His glory shall be seen.*

Hymn: "He Leadeth Me"

46 BRAGGART

Central Aim: To distinguish between the boasting that is true and that which is false.

Prelude: "He Included Me"

Call to Worship: "My soul shall make her boast in the Lord: the humble shall hear thereof, and be glad."—Ps. 34:2

Hymn: "All the Way My Saviour Leads Me"

Scripture: Psalm 94:4

Prayer: Our Father in heaven, take the natural urges of our being and purify them to the praise of Thy glory and goodness.

MEDITATION

It is a common trait of humanity to boast. We want to be just a little bit superior—not much, but a little. Or we want to have something that costs just a little more than that of our friends. Or we want to know a few more important people than somebody else. Some people like to brag about their accomplishments. They are like the flea who said to the

114

elephant, "Boy, we surely did shake that bridge when we crossed over it." For in truth, almost all we ever achieve is done so in cooperation with others.

Some people like to brag about their strength, or knowledge, or wealth, or position. Since bragging is a natural tendency, is there anything of which we can boast? Yes, for there is a boasting which is false and a boasting which is true.

We cannot boast of what we have done or plan to do. "Boast not thyself of tomorrow, for thou knowest not what a day may bring forth" (Prov. 27:1). Abner promised to deliver a kingdom to David, but he could not insure his own life for an hour. Haman preened himself on the prospects of the queen's banquet, but was hanged like a dog before night. The fool's soul was required of him on the very night he was planning worldly projects for years to come.

We cannot boast of our material possessions. "They that trust in their wealth, and boast themselves in the multitude of their riches; None of them can by any means redeem his brother, nor give to God a ransom for him" (Ps. 49:6-7). Voltaire wrote, "When it is a question of money, everybody is of the same religion." That is not true, however. Did Jesus and Judas have the same outlook on wealth? Did Moses and Balaam see eye to eye on wealth? Did Simon Peter and Simon Magus have the same concept of wealth? Did Zacchaeus and the rich young ruler concur on wealth? Did Barnabas and Ananias have the same disposition toward wealth? In the midst of all that money can buy we must remember that it cannot buy faith in God, unselfishness of inner life, inner resources of power, high quality of character, or discipleship to Christ.

But there is a boasting which we can and ought to do. *We can and ought to boast* in the Lord. "My soul shall make her boast in the Lord: the humble shall hear thereof and be glad."

We can and ought to boast in the Christian progress of

others. "For I know the forwardness of your mind, for which I boast of you to them of Macedonia, that Achaia was ready a year ago; and your zeal hath provoked very many" (II Cor. 9:2). Paul was proud of the progress made in the church at Corinth. So can our hearts rejoice and be proud of those in whom the Spirit of God is evidently at work.

Yes, we are prone to be braggarts. But our faith accepts this root principle of human nature and purifies it. It challenges us to see who will give the most, do the most, suffer the most, inspire the most for the common advantage of all. Therefore "let us consider one another to provoke unto love and to good works" (Heb. 10:24).

Hymn: "He Leadeth Me"

47 TATTLETALE

Central Aim: To show that the Christian must live and practice truthfulness.

Prelude: "More Like the Master"

Call to Worship: "Let your speech be always with grace, seasoned with salt, that ye may know how ye ought to answer every man."—Col. 4:6

Hymn: "I Would Be True"

Scripture: Proverbs 25:11

Prayer: O God, bestow on us the wisdom of Thy truth, and make us creatures of truthfulness for our Savior's sake.

MEDITATION

One of the most common epithets of our childhood is that of "tattletale." When our secrets are exposed or our misconduct laid bare, we feel that someone has snitched on us and we angrily call them what we think they are. Yet many times it is more likely that a "little bird" told it, for we are tattletales on ourselves of what we are or what we think. When Peter denied Christ in the courtyard, he had been identified as one of those with Christ because his speech betrayed him as a Galilean. Inasmuch as our speech does serve as a tattletale on us, what ought we to do about it? Negatively, we could eliminate oaths and slang. "But let your communication be Yea, yea; Nay, nay: for whatsoever is more than these cometh of evil" (Matt. 5:37). Slang and profanity will pepper the speech of a person who has run out of ideas. Many words and exclamations have the aspect of thinly disguised profanity. For example, a dear friend and staunch Christian used the expression, "Well, the great I Am" to express his surprise without ever realizing that in the final analysis it was taking God's name in vain. It takes neither brains nor thought to swear; but to do so shows lack of respect, lack of culture, lack of character, and lack of ideals. In a trial court one day, the judge asked a boy, "Do you understand the nature of an oath?" To which the boy replied, "Of course, ain't I your caddy?" Just so will our speech reveal us.

Negatively, we should be careful about self-praise. "Let another man praise thee, and not thine own mouth; a stranger, and not thine own lips" (Prov. 27:2). Self-praise is like the cackle of a hen. It is a sure tattletale of our self-conceit. We should no more call attention to what we have done than does the bee in making honey.

Neither should we be a gossip-monger. "Where no wood is, there the fire goeth out: so where there is no talebearer, the strife ceaseth" (Prov. 26:20). No truer words were ever spoken than those by Seneca when he said, "It is easier to abstain from a contest than to withdraw from it." Man knows the beginning of sin, but who knows the ultimate issues of gossip?

Nor should we be one of those individuals who feel God-called to monopolize the conversation. "He that hath knowledge spareth his words: and a man of understanding is of an excellent spirit" (Prov. 17:27). Someone has put that into today's expression as "I had rather keep my mouth shut and be thought a fool than to open it and prove that I am."

But on the positive side, our speech is also a tattletale. It reveals our Christian compassion and concern. As such our speech should contribute comfort and encouragement. "The Lord hath given me the tongue of the learned, that I should know how to speak a word in season to him that is weary" (Isa. 50:4). We all have our seasons of weariness when we are crushed and burdened by sorrow, temptation, sin, or fear. But it is the glory of our faith that we can speak the words that put heart and hope into the tired and broken.

We should offer the sincere compliment but never flattery. "Keep thy tongue from evil, and thy lips from speaking guile" (Ps. 34:13). The oil of appreciation applied in a compliment eases many of the frictions of life. A sincere compliment is like a drink of cool water that refreshes, but flattery is like cologne—to be smelled of but not swallowed.

We all resemble the two women who boarded a plane and said to the pilot, "Now please don't travel faster than sound. We want to talk." We all want to talk. And the nature of our talk is telling its tale about us, revealing us for what we are and how we think.

Hymn: "Just When I Need Him Most"

48 RECYCLED

Central Aim: To explore the transformation that occurs with our glorification.

Prelude: "At the End of the Way Is Jesus"

Call to Worship: "Behold, I show you a mystery; We shall not all sleep, but we shall all be changed, In a moment, in the twinkling of an eye, at the last trump: for the trumpet shall sound, and the dead shall be raised incorruptible, and we shall be changed."—I Cor. 15:51-52

Hymn: "Face to Face"

Scripture: Romans 8:29-30

Prayer: Lord, we thank Thee that we will not always be as we are, but rejoice to know that someday we will reach that ultimate perfection promised to those who believe.

MEDITATION

In our ecology minded time, we have become aware that ours is a wasteful generation. Natural resources are consumed at a terrific rate with not much thought for ways of reusing the discarded products. But now, alerted to the problem, recycling has become the word. Use waste paper over again. Make roads out of glass. Change a used product into something else.

From the beginning God has planned this for man. God has never been in the business of creating souls to see them pop like soap bubbles. God has destined us to grow in the likeness of Christ. This growth begins the moment of our salvation and continues until we reach the ultimate perfection of being conformed to the image of His dear Son. The process will end only when we are translated out of this world or when Jesus comes again. On the day when a believer is *with* Christ as he is now *in* Christ, he will be a glorified being made over completely after the likeness of Christ.

This process has its beginning in this life. "But we all, with open face beholding as in a glass the glory of the Lord, are changed into the same image from glory to glory, even as by the Spirit of the Lord" (II Cor. 3:18). Almost any country boy can tell you of the worms in a wasp nest that will turn into wasps and fly away. That is known as metamorphosis— the changing of one form into another. So Paul says of believers that a metamorphosis is taking place. It is a change of the very form of our being that will be completed when we stand in the heavenly places.

John wrote: "Beloved, now are we the sons of God, and it doth not yet appear what we shall be: but we know that, when he shall appear, we shall be like him; for we shall see him as he is" (I John 3:2). John realized that what we are now is not what we will always be.

Not yet has God made a public display of the glory that belongs to His children.

Not yet has God shown the inheritance incorruptible, undefiled, reserved for us in heaven.

Not yet is the robe of righteousness or crown of life visible to the eye.

You may have heard the expression "a diamond in the rough." Here and now the child of God is a diamond of faith still in the rough. But by and by, when his glorification is completed, he will emerge as being cut and polished. Then the reflecting facets of his perfection will flash the fire of the glory of God.

All of this is to be accomplished through the power of God, "who shall change our vile body, that it may be fashioned like unto his glorious body, according to the working whereby he is able even to subdue all things unto himself" (Phil. 3:21). He who is able, who has the power to subdue all the universe to Himself, will raise us up to be with Him in glory. That was the belief of Benjamin Franklin, who composed his epitaph which says:

> *The Body of Benjamin Franklin—Printer*
> *(Like the cover of an Old Book, its contents torn*
> *out and stripped of its lettering and gilding)*
> *Lies here, food for worms.*
> *Yet the work itself shall not be lost*
> *For it will (as he believes) appear once more*
> *In a new and more beautiful edition,*
> *Corrected and amended by the Author.*

Recycling is not new. It is old, as old as God Himself who has been practicing it for generations.

Hymn: "Shall We Gather at the River"

49 THANKS A LOT

Central Aim: To revive and enrich the grace of gratitude.

Prelude: "Come, Ye Thankful People, Come"

Call to Worship: "Serve the Lord with gladness; come before his presence with singing"—Ps. 100:2

Hymn: "Serve the Lord with Gladness"

Scripture: Revelation 11:17

Prayer: Father, we thank Thee for all Thy creation, and for all Thy graces bestowed on us. May the wonder of a grateful heart be acceptable in Thy sight.

MEDITATION

The God-given grace of gratitude is one that can never be exhausted. God is to be thanked for what He has done, for what He is doing, and for what He will do. This expression of gratitude may take many forms, but the ultimate way to say or express thanks to God is to acknowledge in your life that your blessings are God's benefits to you. Whether partly through your own efforts or the efforts of others, the real source of our blessing is God. No one has ever felt the deficiency of human language so acutely as those who have a grateful heart.

Let us thank God for the past. The children of Israel were grateful for their heritage and gloried in a recital of the mighty acts of God. They thanked Him for the patriarchs who had followed God at His call, for the prophets who had the word of the Lord revealed to them, and for the sweet singers of the psalms who poured forth praises to God. At this Thanksgiving time we too are grateful for this heritage and for our national heritage going back to the Pilgrims. Our religious freedom is an inheritance from these hardy souls who risked all to come to a strange land where they could worship God according to the dictates of their conscience. How then will we show our gratitude for such a blessing? By exercising that freedom to worship in frequent and faithful worship.

Let us thank God for the present. The psalmist exclaimed, "This is the day which the Lord hath made; we will rejoice and be glad in it" (118:24). It is good just to be alive, to have a place to call home, a family to be a part of, friends to fellowship with, work to do, challenges to conquer, hobbies to fill our hands, a sense of vitality, and a purpose for being. Certainly our times are difficult, but there have never been any "good old days." Every generation has had its times that try men's souls and cast dark shadows of doubt and despair.

122

On a plaque in a chapel outside of London these words are engraved:

> *In the year 1653 when all things sacred throughout the nation were either demolished or profaned, Sir Robert Shirley, Baronet, founded this church; whose singular praise it is, to have done the best things in the worst times ~~and hoped them in the most calamitous~~.*

This is our day and if we have received the salvation of our souls then thank the Lord and show gratitude by making known to all men everywhere the good news of Christ. Gratitude to God for all that is ours will find its expression in our dedication and commitment. This will be different for different people in different opportunities. Phillips Brooks said, "No man has ever come to true greatness who has not felt in some degree that his life belonged to his race and that what God gives him He gives him for mankind."

Let us thank God for the future. Perhaps you have heard someone use the expression "What is this world coming to?" Well, we don't know all the details; but we do know that God has structured the world for a purpose and in His own way He will complete that purpose. All things will turn to the praise of His glory. In his glimpse into the future, John saw that regardless of how things appeared, God was in control of the future as He had been of the past. Beyond the chaos of this sinful world, beyond the sufferings and disappointments of this earthly pilgrimage, beyond our blundering mistakes, there is a bright, new day.

Thanks a lot, Lord, for just being Yourself.

Hymn: "Praise Him, Praise Him"

50 GIVE AND TAKE

Central Aim: To create an awareness of the true Christmas spirit.

Prelude: "There's a Song in the Air"

Call to Worship: "Wherefore he saith, When he ascended up on high, he led captivity captive, and gave gifts unto men."—Eph. 4:8.

Hymn: "I Gave My Life for Thee"

Scripture: Matthew 2:11

Prayer: Father in heaven, lead us to remember at this time the greatest gift that has ever been given us. Make our hearts rejoice in knowing Thy Gift on Thy tree.

MEDITATION

Although in truth the giving of Christmas gifts is pagan in origin, it has gained a deep significance because of its link with God's great gift so visible, so tangible, and so precious. Christ Himself is our greatest Christmas present. The first note of material gifts at Christmastime was struck when the Three Kings, or wise men, came bearing gifts of frankincense, and gold, and myrrh. As we allow the Christmas spirit to take possession of us, we find again the truth that it is more blessed to give than to receive. Indeed, Christmas is a season of give and take in which we discover that it is not the selfish but the sacrificial spirit that is the most happy one. What can we do in this matter of giving and taking?

Well, we could let Christmas be a time for giving up sin, bad habits, and selfish pleasures. The two words which decisively spell out the meaning of Christmas are *sin* and *Savior*. These two words stand for the tragedy of man and

124

the love of God. Our world is in trouble today because it has not listened to nor believed the message of Christmas. Too many hearts are now, and always have been, set on a car instead of the star, and on money instead of mercy. Too many others have looked on Christmas as an eraser that wipes clean the selfishness and inconsideration of the past twelve months.

Lawrence Houseman tells how in staging a nativity play in London, a concealed bulb was placed in the manger to create an illusion of the heavenly radiance. After the visit of the shepherds and Magi came a scene in which the house lights were all to be turned off. This would focus all eyes on the manger and hopefully lead to meditation on the mystery of the incarnation. But the stage manager made a mistake and cut off all the lights. Out of the silence and darkness a hoarse whisper came, "Hey there, you switched off Jesus." Just so, it is easy in our lives for the radiance of Jesus to be switched off by our carelessness and neglect.

We could let Christmas be a time for real giving, not a mere exchange of presents. "What can I give . . ." is a question often heard at this season. We could give forgiveness to our enemies; tolerance to our neighbors; ourself to our families; a good example to all children; our heart and hand to our friends; compassion to the wayward; loyalty and service to the church; and integrity to ourselves.

But we could also let Christmas be a time for taking. Jesus not only received gifts, He also came bearing gifts of forgiveness, eternal life, and salvation.

We could take Him as teacher. In these last days God has spoken to us by His Son. As in the days of old, let us hear Him gladly, for what He says is so practical we can apply it at once to our own experience, and so straight that we cannot miss the meaning.

We could take Him as our example. In Him is the incarnation of every virtue and the perfection of all obedience.

We could take Him as our Savior and King. It is not enough to have an interest in His birth and coming at Bethlehem. That interest must deepen to a desire for Him to come into the house of our heart. The German folk song is right:

> *Though Christ in Bethlehem a thousand times be born,*
> *If He be not born in you, your soul's forlorn.*

Let us throw open wide the doors of our heart and prepare Him room. And while we sing the Christmas carols and worship the Christ child, let us not forget that God set the example for us in giving.

Hymn: "It Came upon the Midnight Clear"